THE
BLOOMINGTON-NORMAL
CIRCUS LEGACY

THE GOLDEN AGE OF AERIALISTS

MAUREEN BRUNSDALE
& MARK SCHMITT

Charleston   London

THE
History
PRESS

Published by The History Press
Charleston, SC 29403
www.historypress.net

Back cover: Aerial Smiths poster courtesy of Stichting Circusarchief Jaap Best/
www.circusmuseum.nl.
Unless otherwise noted, all images are used with permission from Illinois State University's
Special Collections, Milner Library.

First published 2013

Manufactured in the United States

ISBN 978.1.60949.710.1

Library of Congress CIP data applied for.

Notice: The information in this book is true and complete to the best of our knowledge. It is
offered without guarantee on the part of the author or The History Press. The author and
The History Press disclaim all liability in connection with the use of this book.

THE
BLOOMINGTON-NORMAL
CIRCUS LEGACY

To Don—for making the statements that kick-started this project

CONTENTS

PREFACE

No one cares about this stuff. No one cares about circus history.

These sentences, more than anything else, compelled us to write this book.

As people tasked with overseeing Illinois State University's Circus and Allied Arts Collection in Milner Library, we know that this community, Bloomington-Normal, was home to a rare and exceptional group of performers. They made names for themselves around the globe and lived lives most could only dare dream of. We have met former performers and people afflicted with incurable cases of circus love, and repeatedly, the Twin Cities are spoken of as almost holy ground: Bloomington, home of the Wards; Bloomington, home of the Concellos; Bloomington… Things like the photographs, press clippings, correspondence, ledgers, contracts and films found in Special Collections tell us how vital the circus members of our community were to the entertainment field to which they were aligned.

This book provides an introduction to some of the performers who called the Bloomington-Normal community home from the 1870s to the 1950s. For that time period, homes and winter quarters for these entertainers were here. Yet they regularly left to troupe with circuses where they did unimaginably dangerous things high over the heads of the amazed audiences. They did so because they were artistic athletes known as aerialists. The trapeze was their apparatus of choice, and often its best men and women were towners.

specifically Curtis and his daughter Deana Genders Buckley, gifted us with Tuffy Genders's journals, which provided a wealth of insights. We thank Cliff Horton and Bobbie Therault, who shared their considerable memories of their father, "Pop." Martijn Zegel from Teylers Museum, Netherlands, worked with us to obtain the magnificent poster of the Aerial Smiths. Local luminaries like Denny Watson, Guy Fraker, Fred Wollrab, John and Jan Wohlwend, Don Raycraft, Bill Kemp, Robert E. Handley, Jack Keefe, Ron and Jackie Wohlwend, Dale Sutter, Ruth Eickenberg and Dave and Sharon Blunk gave assistance, guidance and encouragement, and for this, we are thankful. Circus historians Neil Cockerline, David Carlyon, Mort Gamble and David Hammarstrom seemingly always dropped everything to answer questions when they were fast in coming. Chris Berry gamely participated as our "man on the street" in New York City, reporting back to us what he saw and learned at the City Museum of New York City, where so much of the Aerial Smiths material resides. In ways not insignificant, Tony Steele and Al Light fanned the flames of curiosity and guided us on this path. Donna Ward Skura and her son, John Skura, shared the passion for learning more about their fascinating family and also graciously shared their findings along the way. Sarasotans Maggie Concello, the late Bob Snowden and Kenny Dodd encouraged questions and answered them with grace befitting royalty, while Paul and Roberta Ingrassia kept Maureen's body and spirit strong with their support and guidance. Special thanks go to the good-hearted Fred Pfening. Time and again he generously responded to our queries, read drafts and challenged us in ways both frustrating (because there's so much we don't know!) and delightful. Last, but never least, there's family. Without them, we are nothing. For so much more than mere words can convey, thanks and love go to Maureen's family Mitzi and John Brunsdale and Rodger and Anna Singley. Mark would like to extend gratitude to Ben and Claudia Schmitt and Michelle Merfeld.

All these people helped to make this work better. The mistakes are ours alone.

CHAPTER 1
"TRAPEZE FLYING SCHOOL"

Letter addressed to:
"Trapeze Flying School"
Enrollment or Guidance Officer
Bloomington, Illinois, U.S.A.

Postmarked:

Brisbane, Qld Aust. June 21, 1957

L. Peter Molineux
78 Swan Terrace, Windsor
Brisbane
Qld Australia

Dear Sir,

I am deeply interested in a career on the trapeze. As I do not think I have the necessary qualifications to be a flyer, I thought that I might become a catcher. Could you please give me some advice on the subject? I am sixteen and a half, weigh one hundred and forty six (146) pounds, and am about 5'10½–11 tall. I rigged up my own "catch trap" on the wall of the house, but since then we have moved, and I am stranded. Could you tell me

a)   If the game is crowded (more catchers than flyers)
b)   The necessary physical and mental requirements
c)   Any novels or text books which I could lay my hands on
d)   If there are any "flying schools" in Australia
e)   How to go about learning to "catch."
I would be obliged if you could help me out in the above, as it is most
important to me.

Yours Sincerely P. Molineux[1]

Young Peter had lofty goals, likely inspired by seeing the Bloomington-based trapeze performers appearing in the circuses in his native land. This letter was driven by what he believed Bloomington was: the world capital of flying trapeze. For those seduced by circus, it becomes easy to share Peter's vision of what this "trapeze school" must have looked like.

High above, a metal bar creaks; daring young men and women swing through the air holding on to it while they laugh and curse, then curse and laugh, their voices mingling with the distinctive blend of aromas of the sweet-burning wood smoke coming from the red-hot potbellied stove and rank human sweat. The scent wafts to the rafters, where young muscled athletes stand poised on pedestal boards, their wrists taped and rosined so that they can better swoop to make a hand-to-wrist connection with the catcher who is hanging head down on another metal bar called the catch trapeze. Sometimes the leaper falls in tearful frustration into the waiting net beneath him, but if he is able, he always, always climbs back up to try again.

This intriguing and vibrant scene played out inside many practice facilities during the dark and cold winter days in Bloomington. A barn on the east side of town appeared austere, drab and white on the outside, but on the inside, colorful trapeze personnel produced wonders of aerial delight for decades. Some of these artists went on to perform for Peter, and millions of children like him, all around the world. In this way, Bloomington fostered the development of aerial artistry during the early modern period of the American circus, creating flyers and catchers—that elite cadre of trapeze professionals—and formed a tightly knit sub-culture within the broader community. Embraced by some, shunned by others, the flyers within this society maintained grueling winter training and practice schedules to create world-renowned circus performances during the warmer months. No wonder Peter sent his letter halfway around the world. He wanted to learn from the best, and he knew that to get the best trapeze advice, he had to seek out the aerial artists of Bloomington. So did many others.

Peter didn't know that by the time his letter arrived in Bloomington in 1957, the glories of the city's astonishing and storied circus past were fading. But the memories and the stories of the community's circus involvement had started to be collected by a woman, Eleanor Weir Welch, the library director at Illinois State University, determined to save this important cultural heritage. Her work and that of those who followed makes it possible to revisit athletes such as the Green brothers and Fred Miltimore; to learn about Eddie and Jennie Ward, a brother-and-sister team; and to follow the career trajectory of Arthur Vasconcellos, once a ten-year-old truant. In this community hundreds of men and women learned to soar as artists of the air. Here are their stories.

CHAPTER 2

BLOOMINGTON'S FIRST LEAP

THE FLYING LA VANS

B y the mid-1870s, classes in the Fourth Ward School (later known as the Emerson School, and long since demolished) at the corner of Taylor and Evans Streets in Bloomington must have been so engaging as to have inspired daydreams of flight and derring-do in a surprising number of boys, obviously restless and eager to go out and see the world on their own terms. One such set of boys, the Green brothers—Fred, Howard and Harry— arguably set in motion an era that connected Bloomington to the world of the circus for nearly a century and created a legacy to which the city is irrevocably tied.

Sons of a well-known Bloomington confectioner, John Lester Green, Fred and Howard, as reported in a 1928 newspaper, erected a trapeze in their yard for fun, drawing crowds as a result of their increasing skill. The chosen moniker of the Greens' act was the La Van Brothers or, alternatively, the La Vans, a name taken in part from their mother's maiden name of Van Alstine. The exact date of the Green brothers' first public performance as professionals has yet to be discovered, but the September 22, 1877 *Daily Pantagraph*, one of Bloomington's newspapers at the time, published the first documented instance of their involvement with trapeze. "Yesterday evening, a son of Mr. J.L. Green, a lad who is quite a gymnast, fell while practicing on a trapeze and had an arm broken just above the wrist. Dr. Hill adjusted the fractured bones."[2]

It can be assumed that the Green brothers had been working professionally and performing their bar and contortion act as early as September 1877, as

This configuration of the La Van act, consisting of Harry and Amy La Van and Charles Weitzel, worked alongside the great magician and escape artist Harry Houdini on the Welsh Bros. Circus and later Houdini's famous Orpheum Theatre tour in 1899.

and he headed back to Bloomington, leaving aerial performance for good. Howard became a successful attorney and later a judge after receiving his law certificate from Bloomington's Illinois Wesleyan University. He moved to Montana, where he married and raised a family.

After Howard's injury, Fred Green did not waste any time joining forces with fellow show mates Fredericks and Gloss to become the three "Royal

Russian Athletes" or "Fredericks, Gloss and Lavan." So named, they toured in the first six years of the 1880s with, among others, the Batcheller & Doris Great Inter-Ocean Show and the John B. Doris Circus, while also working with William Harris' Mammoth Specialty Company in variety theaters. The Royal Russian Athletes shared the bill with other notable acts like the Siegrist Brothers, performers often credited with bringing the trapeze to North America, while touring with John B. Doris's Great Inter-Ocean Largest and Best Show on Earth. In between circus engagements and at the end of the tented seasons, the trio toured in vaudeville with their trick ladder and horizontal bar acts.[9]

The variety of feats that the La Vans performed throughout their career runs the gamut of the aerialist's trade, from their early efforts on the bar, to ladder acts, to aerial bars and finally to what most would consider a proper flying return act on the trapeze. Bar acts were best suited for a stage and consisted of a ground-based apparatus of two or three horizontal bars, either parallel or uneven, that performers would bound over and swing from, performing all manner of somersaults and contortions throughout. An aerial bars act unfolds the same way as a bar act, but the rigid framed apparatus is suspended in the air, allowing the audience a better vantage point of the performance. A ladders act typically involves performers balancing and doing tricks around, with and through unsupported vertical ladders on the ground. The single trapeze act involves an aerial athlete doing tricks on a swinging bar suspended from a rigging high above the ground, while the double trapeze involves multiple performers interacting between two swinging bars. Finally, the flying return act introduces a catcher hanging upside down on a swinging bar with arms outstretched on one end of the rigging. A flyer or leaper—the term preferred by performers—ascends a rope up to a pedestal board far opposite the catcher. This performer grabs a hanging trapeze bar and leaps off the pedestal board while holding on to that bar. Tricks are performed, or "thrown" as professionals say, upon release of the bar while hurtling toward the hands of the catcher. After being released by the catcher, the flyer returns to the swinging bar again, all while performing more amazing tricks of aerial artistry before landing on the pedestal board, where the trick began.

Fred Green traveled to Europe at least twice during the 1880s. He returned from England the last time in the fall of 1888 after a two-year tour of England and the continent.[10] While he was gone, his mother, Harriett, passed away on November 19, 1887.

Tom Kitchen and Amy and Harry La Van as the Flying La Vans, circa 1908.

Introducing Harry La Van

Harry Green, the youngest of the three brothers, was twenty-two in 1888 and had been working independently for a few years as an acrobat, possibly with Bob Curran under the name of the Ashton Brothers. A 1904 newspaper account relates Curran meeting up with his former partner, Harry La Van, whom he claimed he had not seen for twenty-five years. This article details what could be the early independent professional career of an adolescent Harry La Van, beginning in 1879.[11] If accurate, Harry had a career parallel to his older brothers, starting just a few short years after they began performing. Harry was most certainly polished enough as an athletic performer to join Fred and another Bloomington resident, Rudy Schroeder, to create a new flying bar act in 1889.[12]

During the early 1890s, the La Van Brothers began exhibiting their "new flying bar act" before the public. This double trapeze act, as described in the press, consisted of the brothers turning double somersaults "while passing each other at lightning speed in midair."[13]

In 1890, while trouping with the Fulford Overland Show, Fred and Harry Green added Charles Noble, another Bloomington native bound for aerial greatness later with the Fisher Brothers/Flying Fishers. From 1891 to 1894, the La Vans worked on the King & Franklin Shows, Adam Forepaugh's Circus and the Bob Hunting's Show. While with the Sells Brothers Circus in 1894, Harry La Van fell twenty feet during a performance, leaving him with a broken leg.[14] Luckily for Harry, the *Logansport Pharos* of Indiana got it wrong when the paper reported him "fatally injured" by his fall.[15] Fred and Harry moved to Philadelphia, where they worked out a contract to present their act in Mexico City for three months in the fall and winter of 1895. Before heading to Mexico, the brothers worked on Bentley's Old Fashioned Country Circus,[16] where Harry most likely met fellow aerial performer Amy (also known as Anna) Bowers and married her after a brief romance. On the occasion of their fiftieth wedding anniversary, Amy recalled:

> *He looked so chipper swooping through the air, that I told myself "Anna, that's for you." I was so flustered thinking about him that when I went to put on my aerial act I fell and hurt my shoulder. Providence must have had a hand there because unknown to either of us we occupied adjoining rooms at a theatrical boarding house. When he heard of my accident he came and introduced himself, massaged my shoulders, and we were married a week later.*[17]

Then Harry chimed in:

> *Yes, sir, when first I laid eyes on Anna I knew there was the girl for me. I've never been the one to dawdle, so I proposed right off. She said she didn't believe in whirlwind courtships, so I had to wait for seven days. We were married at 4 p.m. and I had to shove off at 9 p.m. from New York for an engagement in Mexico. Left her in her own trapeze act and didn't see her again for 16 weeks. Boy, she really went to town on the flying ring.*[18]

At the completion of the La Vans' stand in Mexico, Fred made the decision to drop out of the act and move back to Illinois. His father, no longer in the confectionery business, tried to convince him to join him as a hotel manager in Peoria, but Fred was unable to make a go of it. By June 1897, he moved to Chicago, where he opened a cigar store. Two weeks later, he was dead. Initially, the diagnosis was a blood clot on the brain, but after treatment, Fred's condition did not improve.[19] It was later reported that he died of uremic poisoning resulting from kidney disease. News of his passing made newspapers from Decatur, Illinois, to Salt Lake City and Oakland.

In 1898, Harry and Amy La Van were working at a tented circus called Welsh Brothers Newest Great Shows in an act called Weitzel, Bard and La Van. It is interesting to note this particular moment in their career because of the other soon-to-be-famous members of the troupe: Harry Houdini and his bride, Beatrice. Houdini was just then standing on the brink of attaining international stardom as a magician and escape artist.[20] Newly under the management of Martin Beck in 1899, Houdini embarked on a vaudeville tour of Orpheum theaters that would prove career defining for his ability as an escape artist. Beck encouraged Houdini to concentrate less on magic and more on escapes.[21] A reconfigured La Vans act consisting of La Van, Amy and Weitzel worked on the

The La Van act billed as "The La Van Trio" played vaudeville throughout the first two decades of the twentieth century.

This Arnold Riegger photograph shows a diving horse act in Danville, Illinois, in 1922 and exemplifies how he was able to capture both the gritty and ethereal, often in the same shot.

The Flying La Vans as they appeared circa 1922. *Left to right*: Neil Callahan, Marshall Brown, Harold Casanova and Harry La Van.

same bill as Houdini during at least one of his fabled Orpheum stands in Kansas City, Missouri, on April 23–29, 1899.[22]

By 1901, Harry La Van had trained Tom Kitchen to be in the act. Kitchen remained through the 1911 touring season and played with the La Vans on six more circuses. The name of the troupe, which changed often, added the Flying La Vans to the mix as early as 1903, when they were with the Campbell Brothers' Consolidated Shows,[23] but would vary wildly throughout the intervening years. At the end of Kitchen's tenure, the troupe joined with another act, creating what was touted as the "only double flying bar and return act in America."[24]

Arnold Riegger, a young man also from Bloomington, became a member of the Flying La Vans in the 1910s. He worked with the troupe for a number of seasons playing dates at fairs and circuses but retired from the act with his love of circus still very much intact. He became a projectionist at three of Bloomington's beloved old movie houses: the Majestic, the Castle and the Irvin. Starting around the time he was with the La Vans, Riegger also became a photographer. He established a following among circus fans for his black-and-white candid photographs of performers and workingmen in the backyards of circuses. His pictures still turn up in the collections of circus fans across the country. With an insider's knowledge of the show and the people who made their living with it, Riegger documented circus scenes by turns gritty and ethereal. His collection of circus negatives was one of the early additions to the Illinois State Normal University's (now Illinois State University) Circus and Allied Arts Collection in Milner Library. Such familiar faces as those of circus superstars Eddie and Jennie Ward of Bloomington's Flying Wards, silent movie cowboy and circus owner Tom Mix and members of the legendary Hanneford riding family were subjects in Riegger's fantastic images.

The La Vans' act persisted for decades, continually working fairs, vaudeville theaters and circuses throughout the world, ending only when Harry and Amy stopped performing in 1937 at the ages of sixty-two and seventy, respectively. In his "retirement," Harry became a booking agent for Pontchartrain Beach amusement park in New Orleans.

Known for years as "Pops" La Van in the trade, Harry La Van died in New Orleans in March 1952. Amy/Anna La Van, as much a veteran as Harry, died less than a year later in Brokaw Hospital, Bloomington. Their bodies are interred in the Green family plot in Evergreen Cemetery in Bloomington, as is brother and founding La Van Brother Fred S. Green.

CHAPTER 3

WORLDWIDE SENSATION

THE FLYING FISHERS

The sheer magnitude of talent that performed for over fifty years in the Flying Fishers aerial act remains astounding. Even though the Fishers did not originate in Bloomington, nor was the act initially composed exclusively of locals, the act came to be inextricably linked to the city.

Acrobat and aerialist Fred Fisher, birth name Horace Frederick Miltimore, was born in Rockford, Illinois, on July 2, 1855, and lived briefly in Bloomington with his parents and siblings during the early to mid-1870s. According to his own account in the *Daily Pantagraph* in 1910, he left town for the sawdust trail in 1871,[25] though no other source supports that date. Records show that Miltimore did perform in 1875 as an acrobat in Smith and Maxwell's Great Western Sensation Shows.[26] The Miltimore family—parents Horace and Susanna and children Horace (Fred), Charles, William, Albert, Addie and Edward—eventually settled in Quincy, Illinois, for an extended period of time. From there, Fred's younger twin brothers, William and Albert, also became circus acrobats.

By 1879, the Fisher Brothers act had exhibited extensively on the variety stage circuit and appeared with the Hilliard, Hunting and Demott Great Pacific Circus in 1879, as well as the John B. Doris Circus, the Adam Forepaugh Circus and the Wallace and Company Circus. Like many early aerialist acts with some longevity, the Fisher Brothers progressed from being a horizontal bars spectacle to a flying return trapeze act. Beginning in 1884, Fred Fisher's twin brothers, William and Albert, performed in their own individual acrobatic acts based out of Quincy, Illinois.[27] John Ahern, another

The Fisher Brothers, circa 1887. *Left to right*: Fred Miltimore, Henry Franz and Charles Noble.

Quincy-based acrobat and horizontal bar performer, worked first with Albert and later William in 1885 and 1886, but Albert briefly dropped out of public performances after his bride, Emma A. Englebrecht, died in 1886, just three weeks into their married life. The next year, Fred and William performed together as the Fisher Brothers in the Adam Forepaugh Circus. In 1887, the *Quincy Daily Journal* published the following:

Adam Forepaugh opens a season of several weeks at the New Olympic, Erastina, Staten Island, June 28th. After closing there a trip west will be made, Quincy being booked for an exhibition. It is generally conceded that Forepaugh has the best show on the road this season. Two of the Miltimore boys of Quincy are with the show as the Fisher Brothers, doing a flying trapeze act; it is probably the finest act of the kind on the road this season. The arrival of the Forepaugh show will be looked forward to with interest, as it is the greatest traveling show of the world.[28]

The actual beginning of the Fisher act's connection with Bloomington began in the early 1890s, when Fred Fisher enlisted Charles Noble, who adopted the professional name Charles Fisher, into the Fisher Brothers. It was commonplace then for performers to take the surname of their act's boss. Years earlier, Charles had left his position as a telegraph operator to take up aerial acrobatics in an effort to overcome asthma. He worked first with two Bloomington flyers, Harry La Van and Ed La Mar. La Van had been Charles's schoolmate. He initially performed as a circus acrobat but later joined the La Van Brothers. La Mar, born Ed Foreman, another Bloomingtonian, also performed as an aerialist with the Fishers. Fred Fisher retired from aerial work after he was injured in a 1900 performance. His partner, Charles Noble, bought out Fred's share of the act, and Ed La Mar was hired to replace him. Fred stayed in the circus business for a few years after stepping down from the pedestal board. He became the equestrian director for the better part of a decade on the John Robinson Circus before leaving show business altogether. He was working as a manager of the Hotel La Crosse Annex in Wisconsin when he died on November 7, 1914, from complications brought on by diabetes.[29]

Charles Noble's younger brother Clyde joined the Flying Fishers troupe in 1904. As a teenager, Clyde had been a jeweler's apprentice, but he readily took to aerial acrobatics. According to Clyde, the Flying Fishers act expanded to include five performers and was retitled as the tongue-twisting Five Flying Famous Fishers. It was featured by Ringling Brothers that season.

In mid-January 1908, only months after completing a season with the Forepaugh and Sells Brothers Circus, Charles Noble, then thirty-nine, took ill and died unexpectedly at his mother's home, reputedly of heart disease. According to the *Bloomington Bulletin*, Clyde and Charles had leased Bloomington's Coliseum to begin winter practice for the upcoming season, when they were under contract with the Barnum and Bailey Greatest Show

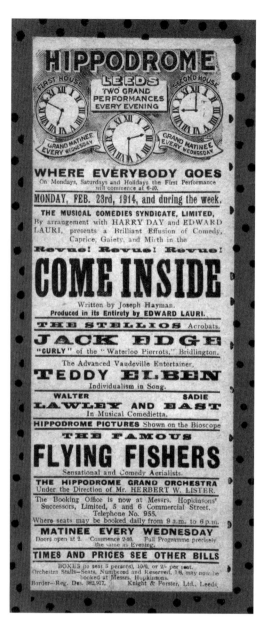

Above: The Flying Fishers as advertised on a 1915 poster for their performance at the Pantages Theatre in Los Angeles, California.

Left: A promotional handbill advertising the Flying Fishers' appearance at the Hippodrome in Leeds, England, in 1914.

Opposite: English lass Emily Vecchi was a member of the Kaufmann Bicycle Troupe. She and Clyde Noble of the Flying Fishers carried on a surreptitious courtship while their respective acts trouped with Ringling Brothers Circus. They later married.

The management of the Flying Fishers eventually came under Quincy's Charles Waller, who, with his Bloomington bride, Edith, kept the act alive. Robert Musselman, Edith's brother, also joined the act. During this period, two Fishers acts toured simultaneously. Charles and Edith Waller's version of the Flying Fishers eventually headquartered in St. Petersburg, Florida, and operated well into the late 1940s with their daughter Connie and her husband, Glenn Higginbotham. The offshoot that Robert Musselman (under the professional name Bob Fisher) created was called Bob Fisher's Fearless Flyers or sometimes Bob Fisher's Five Fearless Flyers. His act included, at various times, many up-and-coming aerialists. For example, Everett White, a solidly built catcher, went on to work with the Flying Concellos, Bloomington's international superstar act of the 1930s and early 1940s. Two more performers from Bob Fisher's act, Bloomington-born Harold "Tuffy" Genders and Gracie Moore (whose first name has been spelled in any number of creative ways), married in 1932 during a performance, standing high on the trapeze rigging's pedestal board at Pennsylvania's Idlewild Amusement Park. Tuffy later worked in Art Concello's myriad acts. He ultimately worked his way up to no less than Ringling Brothers and Barnum & Bailey's general manager, a feat parallel to that of Concello's.

Bob Fisher's aerial act showed extensively in the mid-1930s in North America for a prolonged stint with Russell Brothers Circus and then booked internationally to such far-flung locales as Berlin and Buenos Aires. While the lineup of the Fearless Flyers regularly changed, Bob; his beautiful wife, Frances; and their daughter Maxine remained constants. Images of the act throughout the late 1930s show a family enjoying a life of adventure by doing what they seemingly had been born to do—fly trapeze. But those idyllic days abruptly ceased on December 17, 1940, when Frances Musselman died unexpectedly at age thirty-nine of a kidney ailment and high blood pressure.[34] Bob Fisher's act carried on only for a few seasons more after his wife's death.

In 1950, Clyde Noble published an influential article in *White Tops* magazine, the house organ of the Circus Fans Association of America. "Bloomington Illinois: the Home of 'The Man on The Flying Trapeze'" is a strange account filled with glaring errors, confused chronologies and a mishmash of facts. Normally an account of the origins of Bloomington's circus history from an early participant would be extremely valuable. Noble's skewed history, however, is confounding, with little in it of genuine historic value. Nevertheless, it contains information that otherwise might never have come to light. One such example is Noble's memory of Louis Fitzhenry, yet

Bob Fisher's Five Fearless Flyers. *Clockwise from top*: Bob Musselman (known professionally as Bob Fisher), Frances Musselman (Fisher), Rose Fleming and Herb Fleming. Ray Hendryx is in the center.

another Fourth Ward School pupil, who, like so many others, was beguiled by circus acrobatics. Noble notes that Fitzhenry's parents thwarted their son's plan to run away with the circus to become an aerialist. Instead, he grew up to become a one-term congressman from Illinois and later was known by the esteemed title of Federal Judge Louis Fitzhenry. Judge Fitzhenry's papers (which include, believe it or not, his moustache!), held in the Jo Ann Rayfield Archives of Illinois State University, substantiate the account through correspondence with his former schoolmate Harry Green of the Flying La Vans.

THE MINNIE FISHER QUANDARY

Minnie Fisher played a strange role in the story of the Flying Fishers. No documented legal evidence of a marriage can be found between Charles Noble and Minnie Averiett. Admittedly, marriage records from the late nineteenth century are spotty and difficult to track down. Contemporary newspaper articles noted Charles Fisher performing with his wife, Minnie (Noble) Fisher. Circus posters and programs certainly promoted her as both

Advertisement for the Five Fearless Flyers diagramming a few of their remarkable aerial feats.

"Minnie Fisher" and "Minnie Noble." She was an aerialist and an equestrian, often performing as both on the same circus. When Charles Noble died suddenly in 1908, the event was more than adequately covered in the local press. Newspapers of that time tended to mention grieving widows and widowers, at least in passing. It is curious that Minnie was never mentioned.

The Flying Wards, Jennie and Eddie Ward (on left), with fellow Bloomington performers Mary and Gene Enos.

No matter how their trapeze act started, they stayed with it and excelled, eventually developing a spectacle worthy of a paying audience. The *Atlanta Argus* reported their first verified performance on September 3, 1903: "The Flying Wards, two young people, did a very clever act upon the trapeze. This feature is much better than the average of such acts and it will be repeated each day of the fair."[35]

Recalling the Flying Wards' early performance in Illinois, Eddie Ward told journalist Earl Chapin May that they were paid $15 for their weeklong contract at the Atlanta Fair, but they also decided to pass a hat around to the spectators, and in that way they earned more than $450[36] (in today's dollars, that would be the equivalent to collecting over $10,500). Eddie,

Jennie Ward early in her professional career, circa 1911.

understandably swollen with pride, presented his mother that hatful of cash, a fortune, whereupon she told him to quit the butcher shop and newspaper jobs immediately. From that point forward, Eddie and Jennie were professional trapeze performers.

The next year, the Flying Wards repeated their weeklong stand at the Atlanta Fair with an act presumably even more polished than their 1903 debut. In 1905, Eddie and Jennie secured work with the C.W. Parker Amusement Company, a major carnival, where they did a double trapeze act. Additionally, Jennie was asked to perform for an injured woman named Demona in a loop-the-loop act that is nearly beyond comprehension: Jennie climbed to the top of a thirty-foot-tall platform, where, with much fanfare, she was locked into a hollow wooden ball. The ball was then pushed down a steep incline, gaining the momentum necessary for it to continue its path inside a large steel loop. Revolving constantly, up to sixty-six times in six seconds, the ball hit a much smaller incline after circling the loop, where it left its steel supports, hurtled through space and landed in a net many feet away.[37] Once the ball hit the net, a spring released the girl from the ball, and she descended gracefully from the net to the ground below.[38] In one of her first interviews, Jennie described her experience:

> "We have to take chances," she said simply…"But the loop is harder than it appears. I get whirled over so fast, and the turns are so short, and then sometimes I strike in the net on my head, sometimes on my back. And then sometimes the net gives too much and I strike the ground. It is always a pretty hard jolt, then of course I brace myself inside the ball, and this makes it worse when I strike something solid. But it doesn't happen often."

This article presents a vivid description of the petite and daring star:

> Miss Ward is smaller than the usual Miss of 15, but her arms are like strands of hempen rope, so solid is the muscle developed by her occupation. She is very dark with hair and eyes coal black. But her face is older in expression than her years, the effect of the nervous strain under which she exists.[39]

By the end of their 1905 season with the C.W. Parker Amusement Company, little Jennie was no longer performing the "Girl from Abilene" trick in the ball because Demona had recovered enough to get back into the business. By then the Ward siblings had gained enough skills and showmanship to sign a

Eddie Ward (looking out of place in a suit) while in Cuba to perform with the Flying Wards, 1917.

Eddie Ward and his wife, Mayme, in the circus backyard around 1921.

contract for 1906 with the prestigious Ringling Brothers Circus. They spent the 1907 season with the Van Amburg Circus, but contracted again with Ringling between 1908 and 1912.

In 1913, Eddie Ward built the first of two training barns. The first was located on the eastern outskirts of Center Point, Iowa. Designed specifically for practicing their act, this barn touted "The Flying Wards" on its outside walls in letters several feet tall.[40] For two years during the off-season, the Wards gave performances in this barn for their friends and neighbors. The members of the Six Flying Wards performed in acts ranging from acrobatics to clowning to trapeze, while a visiting troupe, the Pachecos, entertained the crowd laced with fans from as far away as Chicago with wire walking, acrobatics and clowning. After all the seats had been filled, boys and men climbed to the roof supports and overhead beams to watch the spectacular feats while the three-piece band (piano, violin and drums) accompanied the performances.[41]

During their Iowa period, the Wards' simple brother-and-sister act expanded to include more performers, incorporating members of the Hines-Kimball Troupe (Eddie married Mayme Harvey in 1912; they stayed together until his death in 1929); the Hubbell Sisters Mabel, Jessie and Erma (Mabel later married silent movie cowboy and circus impresario Tom Mix); Alec Todd from the Flying Herberts (who married Jennie Ward in 1912); and others whom Eddie introduced to flying. The Flying Wards toured Central America and performed on the vaudeville theater circuit back in America. In vaudeville, performing in smaller venues and on stages, the act often pared down to consist of only Eddie and Jennie. Reviews of their performances continued to rave: "The Flying Wards opened the bill with an aerial act which proved a real sensation. The man and women work as fast as chained lightning and one hazardous trick follows another so quickly that one is amazed and bewildered by the reckless daring of the artists."[42]

Eddie described the reasons behind their speed:

> *We come on the stage, go through our act as rapidly as we can and get off. There is less than a minute during the entire time when we are not busy, and we never play to the galleries or let the audience know that we are asking for applause. Of course we like to have our act appreciated and applauded, but we never play for it and no matter how much applause we get we never "take a bow" or anything of that sort.*[43]

The Iowa barn foreshadowed the one Eddie built on the outskirts of Bloomington. He constructed the much-celebrated barn at 1201 East Emerson Street in 1915. This structure was seventy-seven feet long, forty feet wide and thirty-eight feet high. The floor was eighteen inches below grade, giving an internal height of nearly forty feet, similar to the heights achieved under the canvases of circuses. Twenty-two windows brought natural light into the structure, twenty of which were six feet high and twenty-four inches wide, nine feet off the ground. Interior supports were made of three- by ten-foot planks, with six on each side of the barn. On each of these twelve supports, step-boards were nailed so that children could acclimatize themselves with altitude or simply gain a better vantage point for watching flyers practice. Aerial rigging was anchored to rings embedded in the floor in four locations, two at each end of the facility. Additional pairs of rings were installed in the walls of these ends. A net, nearly as wide as the building, extended over the entire length. Beneath the net was a sawdust ring where animals were trained for performance.[44] Pulleys for a "mechanic" were set into the ceiling of the barn. A "mechanic" is piece of safety equipment fashioned like a belt

The Flying Wards performing outdoors on their flying return rigging. Date and venue unknown.

The Flying Wards. *Left to right*: Ernie Lane, Mabel Ward (Hubbell, and future Mrs. Tom Mix), Erma Ward (Hubbell), Eddie Ward, Jessie Arbaugh (Hubbell) and Bert Doss.

that fits securely around a flyer's waist. Ropes are attached on either side of the belt, passing through the ceiling pulleys on both sides of the net. A more expert aerialist held the ropes from the floor to assist new flyers in falling properly to the net. Thus, a trapeze school was born.

The act spent the touring seasons from 1914 through 1919 with the popular Hagenbeck-Wallace Circus, performing through several of those winters in Cuba. They toured the United States with the Sells-Floto Circus from 1921 through 1928, while Eddie's flying trapeze school acquired a nationwide reputation for minting extremely skilled flyers.

Several of the Flying Wards' thrilling feats made them stand out from other trapeze acts. One was the seemingly impossible foot-to-foot catch. In this daring trick, Jennie positioned herself on a trapeze bar above Eddie, who sat or hung with legs extended outward on a trapeze bar directly below her. Jennie would drop headfirst from her bar to pass her brother—a trick demanding split-second timing—locking feet with him.

They did this trick with incredible speed and while forty feet in the air with no net beneath them. A 1909 *Hampton's Magazine* article described Jennie's attitude toward her career:

> *"There is the young woman who is afraid to cross a railroad track!" It was Mrs. George Hartzell, wardrobe mistress of one of the big tent shows, who spoke. I turned to see the girl on the edge of the group in the dressing room door, the girl I had just observed in the daring trapeze leap. She was in street costume now and had dropped the picturesque, "Mademoiselle" of the circus program for plain "Jennie Ward," a light-hearted whole-souled American girl of 21, who blushed very easily and very prettily.*
>
> *"Who wouldn't be afraid of a great big engine?" she demanded indignantly. "I don't see why you should have anything to fear because you are jumping thru [sic] the air. I know that my brother will catch me, that he must catch me. On a railroad track I haven't any assurance that a train won't run over me. I might fall before I get across or my foot might catch in the rails, or—why, there's all the difference in the world."*[45]

A TIMELINE DOTTED WITH TRAGEDY

Eddie and Jennie Ward enjoyed nearly twenty bittersweet years as the nucleus of the Flying Wards aerial troupe, a period in which growing fame and success paralleled tragedy after tragedy. *The Billboard* reported on August 19, 1911:

> *"Falls from High Trapeze."*
> *Grand Island, Neb., August 10 (Special to the Billboard). Miss Jennie Ward, one of the Flying Wards, high trapeze artists with Ringling Bros.' Show, fell from the top of the tent during the afternoon performance here last Thursday. Since the team worked without netting of any kind, she fell with great force to the ground and is said to be probably fatally injured internally.*
>
> *She was performing with her brother, who missed his calculations in one of their more daring stunts and the young woman slipped through his legs. Miss Ward was hurriedly removed to the hospital.*[46]

This report indicates that Jennie had fallen while attempting the Flying Wards' signature foot-to-foot catch, hurtling headfirst to the tanbark below with such force that her neck and back split the wooden ring curb upon impact. Eddie later described Jennie's back as having been "bowed like a horseshoe" as a result of her injuries. Jennie survived, he stated, by putting herself through grueling self-devised physical therapy. She would pull herself up on the staked circus tent ropes a little more each day, hoping to straighten her back and regain her strength. By sheer force of will matched with equal heartiness, she flew with the act again the following year—at least, that is one of the more popular versions of the story, the one that Eddie Ward told. As it turns out, however, Jennie most likely fell as a result of a tooth breaking. The *Grand Island* (Nebraska) *Independent* reported the day following the accident that Jennie had fallen while performing a trick popularly known as the Iron Jaw as she was suspended in the air only by a leather strap clenched in her teeth. Eddie, from his position on the bar above, would have been holding the strap as Jennie dangled in space, with nothing more than her bite keeping her there. When her tooth broke, Jennie lost hold of the strap and did, in fact, fall thirty to forty feet to the sawdust below, but the newspaper

The Ward practice barn, built in 1915, at 1201 East Emerson in Bloomington, Illinois, shown here decades later.

reports that she didn't hit the ring curb, as Eddie recalled in the years following. Instead, the newspaper stated that she landed a foot from the ring curb that supposedly deformed her back. It would seem that the story was exploited for all of its power as a lesson about the perseverance of the human spirit. Jennie sustained no broken bones in the accident but did have severe bruising on her back and face. Only two days after the accident, Jennie felt well enough to appear cheerful to the press, expressing her wish to rejoin the show in a matter of days.[47] But Jennie's days were numbered.

She met her awful fate in 1918. The infamous Hagenbeck-Wallace Circus train wreck on June 22, 1918, claimed her life and the lives of eighty-five others, including her troupe mate in the Flying Wards, Bessie Katrenke. Many more were injured. Early that morning, a troupe train whose engineer was asleep at the controls slammed into the Hagenbeck-Wallace Circus train stopped on the tracks at Ivanhoe, Indiana, just outside Hammond. The troop train sliced through the stationary circus train, buckling its cars, and soon after, the wreckage began to burn, dooming those trapped inside to fiery deaths. "Eddie first dragged out his wife and then succeeded in bringing out the dying five-foot, two-inch form of his younger sister Jennie. She expired shortly after being dragged from the wreck, presumably from shock as there were no injuries to the body discoverable."[48] The *Daily Pantagraph* quoted Eddie the next day: "I saw the flames creep on them and hear their maddening cries. They ring in my ears in this quiet hospital ward. They will always ring in my ears."[49] While most Hagenbeck-Wallace personnel were interred in Showmen's Rest at the Woodlawn Cemetery in Forest Park, Illinois, Jennie Ward's body was brought back to Bloomington for burial at Park Hill Cemetery.

Tragedy again struck the Flying Wards in 1921 with the curious death of star flyer Ernie Lane. While practicing with the Sells-Floto Circus at the Chicago Coliseum, Lane missed his triple somersault and landed in the safety net below, but something had gone fatally wrong. Shortly after his fall to the net, Lane felt unwell and returned to his hotel room. The next day, he died in a Chicago hospital, likely due to a brain injury. He left behind his young wife and infant daughter. Ernie Lane is also interred at Park Hill Cemetery, close to the graves of the Wards. His five-year-old daughter, Helen, rests forever next to him.

It's a wonder that Eddie kept flying, but fly he did. Questioned about his career repeatedly in later years, he replied in Bloomington's *Daily Bulletin* on December 4, 1927:

The Flying Wards standing in the net inside their practice barn on Emerson Street around 1917. *Left to right*: Ernie Lane, Billy Summers, Eddie Ward, Mayme Ward, Jennie Ward Todd and Alec Todd. *Courtesy of Steve Gossard.*

Why does a man want to be president of the United States? I was in the 1918 railroad wreck near Gary that killed my sister and another girl in our company and jammed up everyone else in the act. I've hung my head downward longer than any man on earth. I own my home in Bloomington and I own a farm near Cedar Rapids, Iowa.

I don't have to dress in tights and do stunts for the towners twice a day in all kinds of weather. I don't have to put a level and tape lines on my riggings to be sure they are hanging straight. I don't have to figure on gravity day in and day out. I don't have to do a lot of things that are difficult, dangerous and sometimes disagreeable. But a fellow gets a kick out of doing any star act, in a circus or out of it. It's great stuff while it lasts.[50]

The final blow to the original members of the Flying Wards came with the mysterious death of Eddie Ward in 1929, while the act was performing with the John Robinson Circus in Muncie, Indiana. Details remain scant, but intrigue runs rampant. After Eddie performed one day and died the next, heated speculation ranged from sudden heart failure to syphilis and to the exotic theory of arsenic poisoning. Circumstantial evidence exists for each theory. Because the cause of Eddie Ward's death was not obvious, an inquest was performed in Muncie, but the Delaware County, Indiana coroner's inquest files for 1929 have gone missing. The certified death record for Edward W. Ward lists his primary cause of death as acute hepatitis and acute nephritis.

By 1929, the two founding members of the Flying Wards were dead, both before their time.

THE FLYING WARDS' LASTING LEGACY

The crucial decision to create a trapeze practice facility in Bloomington is the cornerstone of the Flying Wards' legacy. Through their hard work and foresight, the reputation of the Flying Wards outlasted its founders. In numerous name iterations and lineups, the act continued to exist for well over a half century, playing dates with circuses, theaters and fairs around the world.

Built in 1915, the Ward training barn was a clearinghouse of the aerial arts, bridging the gap between seasoned professional performers and eager young neophytes. It was not unusual for an established act of the stature of the Flying La Vans or the Flying Fishers to book time to hone its craft in this one-of-a-kind structure where countless circus careers began. As a child, long before he was a flyer, Bert Doss helped carry wood to build that iconic structure for the sole payment of being able to bounce in the flyers' net. A few years later, Doss and his future wife, Agnes, trained as flyers in the Ward barn,

Fannie Ward with her daughter Jennie Ward on right. Unknown woman at rear.

just as Harold "Tuffy" Genders and Arthur M. Vasconcellos began their professional careers there after being initiated into it in Bloomington's legendary YMCA facility. Vasconcellos, as a member of the Flying Wards, changed his name to Art Concello and became a trapeze artist of notable fame—a natural flyer who could perform a triple somersault with great consistency.

Concello's talent extended beyond the bar and net to include the management of the barn. Through him, the Wards' legacy continued to resonate, as the site became an industrial operation known the world over for creating first-rate aerialists who could make their way to any point on the globe to perform at a moment's notice.

Chapter 5

Spirit, Mind and Body

YMCA

Circus performers were used to "trouping"—traveling from town to town, usually up to forty weeks at a time—starting in late April or early May. In the fall, at the conclusion of the American circus season, many of the aerialists returned to Bloomington because of its central location, its comparatively inexpensive cost of living, its training facilities and its good transportation/railroad service. When they reentered the community, they probably spent time relaxing and perhaps even more time reconnecting with family and friends they had not seen during the long, hot trouping days. If they wanted to continue their show business careers, they spent this downtime practicing in various Bloomington venues to improve their routines. They also often used the time to cultivate new talent for their acts as well. And sometimes they performed with and for the locals.

Beginning in 1900, the Traveling Men's Protective Association, known locally and nationally then as the TPA, hosted an annual minstrel show that occasionally included circus acts like the La Vans' triple horizontal bar act that closed the 1902 TPA show.[51] This event changed venues regularly, sometimes using the Coliseum and sometimes the Grand Opera House. The Coliseum housed the TPA's vaudeville presentation in 1910, but its *Pantagraph* review proves tantalizing yet oblique because, if accurate, the Flying Wards' first public performance had been held years earlier:

> *The opening and sensational act of the bill first presented last night at the Coliseum is a daring aerial act by the Flying Wards. Mr. and Miss*

The YMCA building in Bloomington, constructed in 1909 and seen here about ten years later.

Ward are Bloomingtonians who were born and raised here and will be remembered by many as the boy and girl who used to practice on the trapeze at their home on South Madison Street in this city a number of years ago. The first public performance in this city, it will be remembered, was a special feature in connection with one of the annual TPA minstrels held here about eight years ago.[52]

The Bloomington Young Men's Christian Association's facility, the YMCA, became one of the aerialists' favorite practice venues. The Bloomington chapter of that international organization began in 1878, and with only a few setbacks along the way, the association laid the cornerstone for its very own building on September 22, 1907, at 201 East Washington Street. When that facility was completed in 1909, it boasted such modern features as a swimming pool, a gymnasium, boarding rooms, meeting spaces and offices for a handful of staff. For special events, like its annual circus, the gymnasium's main floor comfortably seated six hundred, and the gallery sat seven hundred.[53]

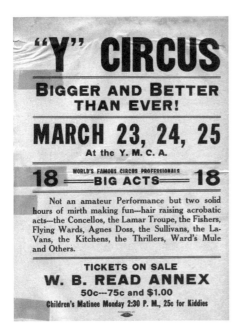

Top: Two tickets to the January 1, 1910 YMCA "Four Claws and Stingling Brothers World's Greatest Circus." The show name was a play on popular circuses of the day, the Adam Forepaugh and Sells Brothers Circus and Ringling Brothers.

Bottom: Handbill advertising an aerial-heavy and star-studded Bloomington YMCA Circus in 1931.

Housing an off-season circus, or using a circus as a fundraiser, was not unique to the YMCA. Shortly after the dedication of the Bloomington Coliseum in 1898, Petersburg, Illinois winter resident Ed Shipp brought his indoor circus to the building. Twenty wagonloads of earth, two loads of cinders and large amounts of sawdust transformed the venue into a circus "minus the uncomfortable seats."[54] Shipp, a longtime performer turned equestrian director for Ringling Brothers and other large shows, began his stationary winter circus in 1888 to meet expenses and help performers like his wife, noted equestrienne Julia Lowande, maintain their conditioning. Harry and Amy Green of the Flying La Vans performed with great success in Shipp's circus in 1901 as "expert aerial gymnasts."[55] About 1,400 people attended the first Bloomington performance of Shipp's Indoor Circus in 1901, and while it was originally slated to run for five consecutive days, its stay was extended for three more to accommodate the crowds.

In 1904, the YMCA hosted a "Carnival of Athletics" at the Bloomington Coliseum years before its circus debuted and before it had its facility large enough for any kind of show. Its events consisted of routines on a pommel horse, parallel bars and springboard. Acts included high dives, pyramid building and tumbling, with such usual athletic competitions as pole vaulting, high jumping and the shot put. The "closing number" was a basketball game.[56]

Soon after its building was completed, Bloomington's YMCA established a show called the Four Claws and Stingling Bros. Circus (a play on the Forepaugh and Ringling Brothers circus titles), which debuted on January 1, 1910. Directed by Lloyd Eyer, the Y's physical director, and presented only twice, at 3:00 p.m. and 7:15 p.m., the show attracted 1,500 spectators to the YMCA, transformed for the occasion to represent circus main and sideshow tents usually appearing in the summer. The *Daily Bulletin* reported that "it would have been impossible to accommodate a larger crowd"[57] because the viewing capacity was 1,300. The program included such city notables as Fred Wollrab, Roy Costigan, Lawrence Rust and Charles and John Brokaw. Arguably the most famous circus flyers of the time, Eddie Ward—living at that point in Iowa—and Clyde Noble, performed unconventional roles with the clown band.[58] Sales of popcorn, peanuts and ice cream in the lobby accompanied the spiel enticing the audience to see the "Water Rat Exhibit," which was actually Bloomington's own 565-pound "Big Boy" Baby Bliss, in the pool after the main show.[59] The afternoon admission cost $0.25 for adults and $0.15 for children under sixteen, while the evening performance garnered a flat fee of $0.25. Performers donated their acts, and after expenses, the YMCA netted $175.00, an impressive sum at a time when the average annual family income was $750.00.

This Bloomington YMCA circus started off with a stutter, perhaps because the first acts were composed entirely of men, keeping with the parameters of the Young *Men*'s organization. By the mid-teens, however, both sexes were plentifully represented, and by the 1930s, women appeared equally with men on the entertainment rosters.

The Four Claws and Stingling Bros. Circus didn't keep its original title for long. By 1924, it was known only as the Y Circus, a name it maintained until its last production in 1941. Performances typically lasted about two hours and consisted of as many as twenty-two acts. A wide array of talented performers dazzled crowds with routines often mixing amateurs and professionals. The famous aerialist Art Concello often paired with Illinois State Normal University's gymnasts and Gamma Phi Circus coach Clifford "Pop" Horton in hand balancing and tumbling acts,[60] sometimes also doing turns in a comedy tumbling troupe with Harold Ward, Eddie Ward's son.[61] YMCA physical director C.D. Curtis hung in the catch trap for both the YMCA Flyers, to which Art Concello and Marshall

Lang belonged,[62] as well as for the combined flying act of the La Mars and the Fishers.[63] Bloomington native Lewis Probasco, a graduate of Illinois Wesleyan University and the University of Wisconsin law school, performed on the same bill as Eldred "Red" Sleeter, another Bloomington product. Sleeter's wife, Mitzi Moore, was Gracie Genders's sister, and both of them had been performing in circuses since they were children.[64] Harold Ramage, an employee of the Keiser-Van Leer hardware store and an all-around friend to many circus performers, performed in the Clown Band.[65] Over the years, a number of local Bloomington luminaries performed as the circus's ringmaster.

Aerial acts understandably dominated the YMCA circuses. The Fishers, Wards and La Mars troupes were only three of the many flying acts that participated. The Billettis, a high-wire troupe, often performed with the show,[66] and the ultra-feminine beauty and muscle grinder Ullaine Malloy, "the Blonde Bombshell of the Big Top," also made frequent Bloomington appearances,[67] eventually becoming a resident. "You really work under pressure here," she explained in a 1938 *Pantagraph* interview. "You see, the top notchers from all over the country come here to perform just for the fun of it and don't think they aren't critical of each other. It does us all good."[68] Other popular acts consisted of teeterboards, the iron jaw, parallel bars, slack wire, aerial ladder and pyramids.

For years the Ward family's contributions to the YMCA circus remained constant. After Eddie died in 1929, his daughter Genevieve Ward displayed her single trapeze and web act there in 1931,[69] and her uncle Elza Ward's mule also put in appearances in 1928 and 1931. Ward protégés were regular performers too and were sometimes billed as "Wards" instead of their other stage names, including Art and Antoinette Concello, Harold "Tuffy" Genders and Mickey King.

The Beagle Troupe introduced multiple animals into the Y Circus in 1938, including dogs, goats, monkeys and black bears. Dick Clemens, a lion trainer from Creve Coeur, Illinois, also brought his lions Patsy and Tyrone to perform for the first time indoors. Captain John Snyder presented black bears walking on stilts, riding bicycles, roller skating and walking upstairs on their front paws in 1940, the last year animals were used at the Y.[70]

The Y Circus also allowed performers to expand their skills or showcase talent not normally exhibited. Often those very top-notchers whom Ullaine Malloy had cited gave the show all it needed to be a hit. Flyer Carl Durbin and Joe Killian, Art Concello's half brother, served as property men in 1932.[71] Red Sleeter, Billy Ward (not Eddie's direct relative) and Tuffy Genders often

YMCA physical director Clarence "C.D." Curtis with star pupil Art Concello. An unknown flyer is on the right.

YMCA Circus performers in 1936. *Left to right*: Eddie Ward Jr., Walt Graybeal, Jimmy Croutcher, Frances Musselman (Fisher), Maxine Musselman (Fisher), Edith Waller, Evelyn Fleming, Gracie Genders, Connie Waller, Antoinette Concello, LaVon Bornhauser, Marian Bordner, Harry La Mar, Warren Lynes, Wayne Larey and Francis "Gooch" Reiner.

performed in an Arab tumbling group sometimes billed as the Ali Ben Hassan Troupe, not to be confused with the professional act of the same name that had toured with circuses years earlier. Three collegiate gymnastic performers from Iowa joined the act too, testifying to the show's regional popularity.

In 1936 and 1937, a truly spectacular flying trapeze act appeared at the YMCA with four rigs set up in parallel for four catchers and twelve flyers, something never seen before and rarely since. The Concellos were appearing overseas at the time, but among them, the list of performers in this act is a veritable who's who of the trapeze: Rose Fleming, Connie Waller, Frances Fisher, Maxine Fisher, Gracie Genders, Mitzi Sleeter, Charles Waller, Elmo Fisher, Walter Graybeal, Oscar Fouin, Bones Brown, Bob Fisher, Herb Fleming, Harry La Mar and Clarence Croutcher.[72] The group was made up of performers from several acts: the Flying La Mars, Charlie Waller's Fishers, the Flying Sensations, the Flying Flemings, the Flying Wards and Bob Fisher's Five Fearless Flyers.

The strong relationship between the professionals and Bloomington locals persisted throughout the Y Circus's history. Even while Art Concello was transitioning from flying into circus management, the *Pantagraph* often noted his presence at the Y Circus. One incident candidly captured him as Bloomington's most famous circus son: a girl named Mary, fresh from exiting the arena, was catching her breath after her part in an adagio act, a performance dance that demands great synchronization skill and displays frequent lifts and throws.

> *A short, heavy shouldered young man smoking a long cigar stuck out a calloused paw toward her. "I guess you don't remember me from last year," he grinned, but Mary shot back between gasps, "Oh, yes, I do."*
>
> *"You're getting good," the young man said. "You did a forward this year. You couldn't do that last year. You've been working, and you're swell."*
>
> *Mary beamed. The young man was Art Concello, just about the greatest aerialist in the world.*[73]

Antoinette Concello soaring through the upper reaches of the YMCA gymnasium toward the eager grasp of her catcher.

In exchange for their annual performances, circus personnel received extended complimentary YMCA memberships for training purposes. Physical Director Clarence D. Curtis (typically known as C.D. Curtis), who served in that capacity in the late 1930s and early 1940s, scheduled acts to train from 8:00 a.m. until about 11:00 a.m. and again from 2:00 until 4:00 p.m., when high school activities took over the main gym area. The performers resumed practice from 9:00 p.m. until midnight.[74] Besides practicing at the Y, many of the nonresident single men often rented rooms there, while most of the married nonresident performers stayed at nearby Tilden Hall.

The halcyon days of Bloomington's Y Circus came to an abrupt end. In 1941, the *Pantagraph* celebrated its final performance: "Presenting, ladies and gentlemen, 21 acts (count them—21) of death defying daring on the high trapeze, feats of strength, skilled dancing, gymnastics, acrobatics, tight wire antics, contortionists, fire eating, side splitting clowning, and several absolutely new acts never before seen in Bloomington."[75] This performance showcased the largest cast ever of various acts but was, of course, dominated by the aerialists. Attendance was again good, but at the close of its four-day run, the Y Circus went dark.

C.D. Curtis, so often the impetus behind the later performances, had been called up for the United Service Organizations (USO) just a month before the 1941 Y Circus was held.[76] Curtis's departure, along with the draft of so many young men, sounded the Y Circus's death knell, though it was not soon forgotten. A State Farm agent wrote to Art Concello in 1944, "No word has been received by me from any of the other members of your group for some time, and the last word received from C.D. Curtis was that he was doing fine somewhere in the Middlesouth [*sic*]. The regular YMCA circus has been missed a great deal more than you, who helped to make it a success, can realize."[77] The passing of the Y Circus came quickly, but the community continued to mourn it.

Though the Y Circus was no more, locals still trained at the facility. Lewis Probasco, an attorney by trade, not a professional performer, was well enough conditioned as an aerialist/leaper that he substituted for them when needed. As a boy, he had begun training for fun on the YMCA parallel bars, and as an adult, he kept up the rigorous training that made such work possible. Like so many others, he was trained by C.D. Curtis, a man who was so well respected that flyer-turned-manager Tuffy Genders named his only son Curtis.

In 1955, Harry Melby left his YMCA administrative post, the last of the three most steadfast circus backers, the other two of whom were Eyer and

Wayne Larey, Harold "Tuffy" Genders and Billy Ward repair a net at the YMCA in 1937.

Curtis. Cecil Rowe took over as director, clearing all the circus equipment out of the gymnasium and barring performers from using it. "It's a darn shame," longtime circus performer Mickey King remarked upon returning to the community in 1957, "but Bloomington's home to me." She continued, "I found a home here with circus people after I ran away from my childhood home to join the circus. Whenever I want a dentist or an osteopath, I've got to come back to Bloomington."[78]

Circuses and circus-themed events for the general public, and particularly its youth, prospered in the early decades of the twentieth century. Books like *Amateur Circus Life* and *How to Put on an Amateur Circus* were published, the latter marketed specifically to chairmen of extracurricular entertainment clubs, managers of youth Chautauquas, schools and society folk who "wish to produce a pleasing burlesque affair."[79] In addition, YMCAs across North America—from Texas to Wisconsin, New Hampshire to Washington, Pennsylvania to Winnipeg, Canada—held circus-themed events, and more than a few staged annual performances. A typical production might have

LaVon Bornhauser, Marian Bordner, Gracie Genders and Geneva Amadori (at rear) practicing their aerial ballet routine for the YMCA Circus.

been in Spokane, Washington, where its YMCA Circus hosted only amateur acts. Nevertheless, a local newspaper offered brilliant publicity for the show, touting, "The entire acrobatic, gymnastic, hippodromic and spectacular world has been scoured for the bewitching, beautiful, brilliant and burlesque, and the management offers the greatest and most gorgeous galaxy of artists ever gathered under one roof."[80] Acrobats, clowns and sideshow freaks joined a Roman ladder act, a slide for life and a pageant of nations in each performance of the three-day stand.

When the cornerstone for Bloomington's YMCA was laid in 1907, Vice President of the United States Charles W. Fairbanks heaped optimistic praise on this community effort, foretelling a prosperous future for many young men in the fulsome and progressive spirit of the early twentieth century:

> *The Young Men's Christian Association becomes the rallying center of many wholesome influences. There are gathered in its halls noble Christian men who have some higher ambition than to live for themselves alone. When*

this building is completed, there will radiate from it countless generous and splendid influences, giving an impulse to that which is noblest and best in a great, progressive Christian community.[81]

The Y Circus, with all its glamour and popularity, arose from dedication and hard work and provided the "splendid influence" of wholesome entertainment for thousands of the region's population. The Y Circus endeared itself to circus fans naturally, but it also was a point of pride for all the demographics it served: the residents of Bloomington, the Illinois State Normal University and the circus performers themselves.

CHAPTER 6

AMERICA'S OLDEST COLLEGIATE CIRCUS

GAMMA PHI CIRCUS

THE COMMUNITY TO THE 1920S

From 1880 to 1920, the United States experienced a major population shift. The 1920 census revealed that, for the first time, a majority of Americans lived in towns of over five thousand residents, as mechanization on the farm limited rural employment opportunities. Large numbers of Americans moved to cities for desk and factory jobs. This demographic shift generally meant fewer physical demands on the job and more discretionary time. At the same time, legislation was passed to improve school physical fitness programs because many prospective World War I soldiers had been declared unfit for service. School districts and cities funded gymnasiums and community recreation centers, and countless books and articles promoted methods of producing physically fit citizens. Organizations like the Young Men's Christian Association helped bring healthy lifestyles to many communities.

The YMCA's first American chapter opened in Boston in 1851, bringing the benefits of physical activity to many citizens. The number of Ys soon exploded, as did participation in team sports. On college and university campuses, participation in sports like football, basketball and baseball were initially intramural competitions, many hosted at local Ys. Yet these highly competitive sports did not bring a circus to the Illinois State Normal University. Gymnastics did.

Illinois State Normal University's Gamma Phi Circus founder, Clifford "Pop" Horton, stands atop a young man's shoulders in a detail from an early acrobatic performance in Streator, Illinois.

By the 1920s, the twin cities of Bloomington and Normal were prospering. Eighty passenger trains arrived and departed daily. Interurban rail service made travel to Peoria in the west and St. Louis in the south easy. The town coliseum seated four thousand for large events, while seven theaters offered entertainment ranging from plays to vaudeville performances. Forty churches tended to the spiritual needs of the population. State Farm, a new insurance company, found roots in the metropolitan area, as did other companies such as Country Financial. Twelve ward schools, a central high school and Illinois Wesleyan University fulfilled most of the community's educational needs.

Illinois State Normal University (ISNU), located in Normal, Illinois, a few miles north of Bloomington, was similarly expanding, reaching an enrollment of 1,482 by 1926,[82] and its students demanded more varied courses, necessitating the expansion of academic departments and programs. Physical education proved to be one of the most popular offerings.

THE ROOTS OF GAMMA PHI

Physical education's seeds germinated in the field of gymnastics at Illinois State Normal University. Upon arriving in 1862, Richard Edwards, the school's second president, required all students to participate in "free gymnastics accompanied by music."[83] ISNU employed "Teachers of Gymnastics" by the end of the century until the early 1910s, when the university hired "Physical Education Directors" for both women and men. Clifford Horton came to ISNU in 1923 as an athletic coach and the first full-time teacher of physical education for men. His office, as well as the campus center for the health and physical education program, was in Cook Hall.

Born December 31, 1892, in Shelton, Washington, Clifford Emory Horton was the son of a salesman. When he was a young boy, his parents moved frequently, a common situation for families who were unable to make rent payments, crisscrossing the state of Washington from Tacoma to Spokane, where in 1903 Cliff joined the city's Athletic Club, an organization that emphasized boxing but also offered gymnastics, which became Cliff's lifelong fitness passion. At sixteen, he graduated from eighth grade and entered the new North Central High School, but he never graduated because both of his parents fell ill. In 1911, he went to work as a towel clerk at the Spokane YMCA, where he stayed for two years.[84] He helped produce its circus, which "had a number of acrobatic acts and clowns and was as nearly typical a circus as could be done indoors."[85]

Horton left Spokane's YMCA to become the physical director at the YMCA in Michigan City, Indiana. There he befriended a recent graduate of the International Young Men's Christian Association College, which later became Springfield College in Springfield, Massachusetts. That acquaintance spoke glowingly and near-incessantly of that college's gymnastics program, fueling the deep respect for the field, as Horton explained years later: "Excellence in performance of gymnastics was an essential quality of an individual of the organization. It wasn't to the exclusion of other forms of participation, but at the time gymnastics wasn't the type of thing that was generally promoted. To me, it had a much more satisfying appeal…it just felt good!"[86]

Horton undoubtedly heard many other things from that unnamed Springfield alumnus. He likely learned a bit about James Naismith, the inventor of basketball; something of Luther Halsey Gulick, head of the school's Physical Education Department and the person who developed the YMCA's triangular logo symbolizing mind, body and spirit; and probably most about Springfield's annual "Home Show," a gymnastics exhibition that began there in 1904. Not surprisingly, Horton lit out for that institution at his first opportunity.

While at the International Young Men's Christian Association College pursuing his bachelor's degree in physical education from 1915 to 1919, with a year away to complete his World War I service obligation, Horton practiced gymnastics and studied with fellow student Leslie Judd. Judd graduated the year after Horton did, in 1920, and went on to establish a gymnastic "Exhibitional Team" that traveled internationally. Judd's values— and Horton's—placed importance not on "winning teams and successful exhibitions but rather on the total development of the individual student,"[87] a position that possibly reinterpreted the YMCA philosophy to advance the mind, body and spirit of young men.

Ohio Wesleyan University in Delaware, Ohio, hired the twenty-six-year-old Horton as a part-time physical education instructor before he graduated from Springfield College. In December 1917, he became a member of the Beta Chapter of Gamma Phi, a gymnastics fraternity whose first chapter was formed in 1903 at The Ohio State University.[88] Though new to the eleven-year-old Ohio Wesleyan chapter, Horton pushed its members to put on a gymnastics performance in the style of an indoor circus.[89] The result was the Athletic Carnival of 1918, which showcased men executing routines under Horton's direction on the horse, parallel bars, rings and elephant, a now-obsolete set of parallel bars covered by thin mats over which students would leap from a springboard, performing tricks that became known as "leaping the elephant." Horton's own appearance on the parallel bars and elephant was described as being the "finest ever seen in Delaware."[90] Clearly Horton's

This photograph is an example of the kind of feats of balance and strength that characterized early Gamma Phi performances at Illinois State Normal University.

passion for gymnastics fueled his performance, but he also evidently had something of a romance with the circus.

After completing a master's degree at Clark University in Worchester, Massachusetts, Horton brought this passion to Illinois State Normal University, where he instilled it in the young men who performed tumbling and clowning routines during halftimes of ISNU football and basketball games. These "Pep Artists" were frequently documented in school yearbooks after Horton's arrival. As a natural extension of his interest in gymnastics and circuses, Horton petitioned the university's administration for a chapter of Gamma Phi at Illinois State Normal University, which was granted in early November 1929.

The November 11, 1929 issue of ISNU's student newspaper, the *Vidette*, announced the formidable criteria for acceptance into the gymnastics fraternity:

> *Any man who has three physical education credits is eligible provided he meets all the requirements to become a member. According to the constitution, he*

must have leadership ability, be able to teach gymnastics, strive at all times to have good posture, know sportsmanship code and practice it religiously, do a number of stunts on parallels and horse, have Physical Education grades averaging 80, know the Normal nine, be able to teach ten of the unit pyramids shown in the physical education syllabus for winter term, have voice clarity, and ability to command, pass a physical efficiency test in the following events: first, 100 yd. dash, 12 seconds; second, running high jump, 4 feet 4 inches; third, throw baseball 217 feet; fourth, throw baseball accurately, four strikes out of five; fifth, running broad jump, 14 feet; sixth, punt a football 35 yards; seventh, forward pass accurately to man running in lateral zone; eighth, make 7 out of 10 free throws; ninth, rope climb, 18 feet in 8 seconds; tenth, hand spring successfully.[91]

Though these qualifications were initially tough, they were relaxed to include more gymnastic and circus-oriented skills.[92]

In Gamma Phi's early days, its members made names for themselves not only during halftime gymnastic routines but also in various intramural sports. In the early 1930s, Horton and some of his athletes performed at Bloomington's YMCA Circus in tumbling, hand balancing and pyramid acts alongside many of the circus performers who wintered in the community. This was not surprising, given Horton's deep roots in the YMCA and the intensity with which C.D. Curtis promoted its circus. However, starting in the spring of 1932, Gamma Phi began its own annual circus exhibition, which, like Springfield, Massachusetts's annual gymnastic exhibition, was called its Home Show. The earliest performances in Bloomington took place at the McCormick Gymnasium, built in 1925, on the west side of the campus quad. The first year's performance featured nine acts, not all from the Gamma Phi fraternity. The university band provided the music, while groups from the Women's and Men's Physical Education Departments and the University High School took turns entertaining the crowd with acts and dances. Jake Ward, a well-known Bloomington-Normal community member (unrelated to any member of the Flying Wards) and often ringmaster for the YMCA Circus, served in that capacity for Gamma Phi. Lloyd Eyer, a longtime physical director of the Bloomington YMCA and later affiliated with Read's Sporting Goods, assisted with the annual circus each year by testing rigging equipment and ropes.[93]

Though the Gamma Phi fraternity often featured female acts in its annual circuses, women were not formally welcomed into the group until the 1940–41 season. They chose, however, to crown a Gamma Phi Queen

Illinois State Normal University's Gamma Phi Circus founder, Clifford "Pop" Horton, with a wry and roguish grin.

in 1933. This tradition, which lasted until 1969, was put in place to help "glamorize the circus."[94]

Meanwhile, beyond the university, circus performers continued to make Bloomington their home during the off-season. Occasionally, some of the professionals used the university's gymnasium for practice,[95] and as a result, Gamma Phi eventually produced new acts and procured several pieces of circus equipment. In 1947, Arley Gillett, a Gamma Phi alumnus (1934–38), became its faculty sponsor and coach, a position he held for the next nineteen years. During his tenure, he nurtured the relationship between circus professionals and his students. He explained, "They [the circus retirees] were old circus people and it was in their blood...Everybody wants to teach you his act. It was all they had and they were proud of it. They want to perpetuate it."[96] Gamma Phi thus expanded its inventory of circus equipment to include its first unicycle, rolling globe, perch pole and web.

Gamma Phi experienced several significant developments in its first four decades. Membership shot up after the World War II hiatus, and consequently, the number of acts produced also rose, including tight wire, trick bicycles, roller skating and trapeze. Gymnastic skills and leadership helped Ron Tinsley to become Gamma Phi's first African American president in 1957–58, well before America passed desegregation laws. While no longer the head coach, Horton's thoughts about Gamma Phi and circuses were recorded in the 1956 program:

> *The circus is unique in American life. From childhood it has stood for something wonderful and spectacular, packed full of unusual thrills. Its appeal is universal. Perhaps most of us have at some time or other, in fancy, projected ourselves into the arena to perform feats of daring along with those we watched and admired.*

The Gamma Phi Circus gives students the opportunity to actually experience the thrills and to enjoy the satisfaction of accomplishment along with the admiration of fellow students. College life is rich with opportunities to employ and develop one's abilities, but perhaps nowhere are the opportunities greater than those that culminate in the annual Gamma Phi Circus.[97]

Horton retired in 1961 after a remarkable career. Since the time that Gamma Phi was chartered in Normal, he was called "Pop," an indication of the deep respect and admiration the first Gamma Phi men had for their mentor.[98] The nickname persisted long after Horton's death in April 1981, a week before the Home Show. As is often the case in social organizations, lasting traditions pervade Gamma Phi. One of the most appropriate is that each year before the Home Show, members of the Gamma Phi Circus make a pilgrimage to Pop Horton's final resting place, paying homage to the man who, through their work, continues to bring joy and fulfillment to so many lives. (While many new Gamma Phi initiates are persuaded that

Clifford "Pop" Horton in his office at Illinois State Normal University.

Pop was buried in the classic handstand position, vertically with hands over his head, Pop's son, Cliff Horton, assures us this is not true: "Though, ha!, he sure would enjoy that joke!")[99]

THE LASTING IMPACT

There has not been a great deal of turnover at the helm of Gamma Phi. After Gillett stepped down during the 1967–68 school year, Wayne Truex took over. He was assisted shortly after his arrival by Jerry Polacek, who took the reins in the 1973–74 season. Al Light assumed the role of head coach in 2003 and remained for six years. During his tenure, he brought back to town Tony Steele, a man who became a trapeze legend. Steele first came to Bloomington as a young flyer with Harry La Mar in 1951, when he was fifteen. He later joined the Flying Malkos, and with them he completed his first triple somersault to a catcher in 1955. He was soon performing it consistently. Later, after a stint in the U.S. Army and a return to performing with the Flying Marilees, he completed the previously thought impossible three and a half somersault, being caught by the ankles by Lee Stath. Endearingly, Steele has commented that his time in Bloomington training Gamma Phi members was like a homecoming. Illinois State University and Gamma Phi Circus alumnus Marcus Alouan was named the sixth Gamma Phi head coach in 2010.

Chapter 7

Is There Any Money in It?

Arthur Marshall Vasconcellos and Marie Antoinette Comeau

Circus fans and historians worldwide know Art Concello by reputation or by the nickname "Little Caesar" that he earned as general manager for the Ringling Brothers and Barnum & Bailey Circus. Concello's early life and the remarkable events of his later years, however, don't enjoy a similar familiarity.

Arthur Marshall Vasconcellos was born on March 26, 1911, in Starbuck, Washington, to Arthur B. and Mattie M. Vasconcellos. The 1910 U.S. Census documented his parents twice, once while they lived in Bloomington, Illinois, and again while they were living and working in the state of Washington. Both list his father's occupation as a railroad machinist.

Arthur and Mattie both had Illinois roots. Arthur's Portuguese family hailed from Jacksonville, while Mattie's family originally lived in Sullivan. Mattie brought her two older children, Joseph and Grace Killian, from her first marriage to her second marriage with Arthur Vasconcellos. Work took them west, but according to the 1911 Bloomington City Directory, they maintained their family residence at 801 West Locust Street, where they returned before their youngest son, Art, was a year old.

Young Art's school records are not obtainable, but they would likely reflect his unlimited energy, often directed away from formal academics:

> *In grammar school, which he attended with supreme indifference, being often called on the carpet for smoking cigars during recess, he was noted for*

Art Concello (bottom right). It's hard to believe that by the time this picture was taken, Art had been flying trapeze for three years and was just two years away from joining professionally with the Flying Wards. *Courtesy of the Art Concello Papers, Robert L. Parkinson Library, Circus World Museum, Baraboo, Wisconsin.*

> *his fleetness of foot and his uncommon skill with the shinny stick. In class, he was quick, but unprepared, impatient with an educational system so ceremoniously devoted to the ghosts of departed foreign generals.*[100]

It seems likely that he excelled in extracurricular activities, where he could expend some of his incredible energy. He was a member of the junior basketball squad in 1924–25. There he appears—looking more like a nine-year-old than a teenager—arms behind his back as he was likely instructed to do. He almost looks innocent.

The next year, Art enrolled as a freshman at Bloomington High School. Its annual, the *Aegis*, shows him as an undersized young man caught looking far to the left in the photographs where he appears. Eldred Sleeter, Lewis Probasco and Harold Genders, boys he grew up with and remained his lifelong friends, also appear in that yearbook.

By the time Art was coming of age, Bloomington was producing top-notch trapeze performers like the Flying Wards, the La Vans and the Fishers.

Art Concello appears here as Art Vass in 1928's the Flying Wards.

Practice equipment had sprouted up throughout the community, with rigging in theaters, the Ward practice barn on Emerson Street and the local YMCA.

C.D. Curtis, the physical director of the Bloomington Y, was devoted to developing healthy minds, bodies and spirits, which he had earlier done in Illinois towns Canton and Aurora. Bloomington's Y had been regularly producing a circus in the community since 1910, just as the Wards were swinging their way to international fame. Because flyers were a part of the community's fabric, the Y had well-established rigging, but starting in 1922, Curtis was the first Y employee to train people, especially youths, in its use.

Perhaps one day Art Concello, an undersized ten-year-old, decided school was ancillary to his desires, or perhaps he visited Bloomington's YMCA with the Manual Arts Club, the only school organization he joined. However it happened, Art found himself one day watching Curtis fly on the trapeze. Art wasn't so much entranced by its regular, pendular movement as he was in the potential financial reward for becoming a star performer. He asked Curtis, "Is there anything in it in a monetary way?" Curtis, thinking of the Wards' success, replied quietly, "It's a gold mine."[101]

Art's classmate Harold Genders had grown up on a farm closer to Downs than to Bloomington. His parents, Dean and Maude, owned a home on Grove Street and enrolled their only child in the Bloomington schools. Like Art, he was bright and driven and perhaps also less than enthusiastic about schoolwork. In the high school's Golden Gloves boxing club, Harold earned the nickname "Tuffy," a moniker that stayed with him for the rest of his life.

At the YMCA, Tuffy and Art learned to fly together, tutored by Curtis. After the boys learned the basics—nothing was more important than falling correctly into the net—Eddie Ward, Bloomington's most famous trapeze performer, took them under his wing. Ward, given complimentary membership to the Y in exchange for his gratis performances with its circus each spring, regularly picked up new talent there. With Ward, the boys continued learning new tricks and training until the spring of 1927, when Art upset his family with the news that he was joining the circus as a trapeze performer. He was sixteen.

Eddie Ward's Famous Flying Wards act appeared in the Sells-Floto Circus in 1927, while the act in which Art performed was the Ward-Kimball Troupe on the Hagenbeck-Wallace Circus.[102] Eddie Ward provided flying acts for shows owned by the American Circus Corporation, Ringling Brothers and Barnum & Bailey Circus's biggest competitor. At the end of the 1927 season, Art returned to Bloomington for the winter.

Just then, Antoinette Comeau came to town for the first time with her older sister Mickey. Mickey had married the Sells-Floto Circus's wild animal trainer, Allen King, but by 1927, their marriage was dissolving. The French Canadian Comeau sisters had mostly grown up in rural Vermont

Antoinette Concello in the circus backyard.

Aerialist Gracie Genders in the Ward/Concello practice barn at 1201 East Emerson Street in Bloomington in 1937. Concello completely refurbished the inside after purchasing it in 1935.

Born into a circus family, Alfredo Codona achieved fame due to the skill and grace he displayed in flight. Whatever trick Alfredo accomplished high in the air, he did so with a flair that was simply unmatched. To watch him was like watching the greatest dancer perform in the air with no floor beneath him.

Codona's wife was Lillian Leitzel, another international headliner for the Ringling Brothers and Barnum & Bailey show. She was an acrobat and a consummate flirt, enchanting audiences of all sizes both in and out of the ring. While performing, she was best known for one-armed planges, where she would momentarily dislocate her shoulder while throwing her body up and over a suspended ring she held, encouraging the audience to count the number of rotations (or planges)—often numbering well past one hundred. Together Leitzel and Codona enjoyed such stardom that they were assured year-round work. When they weren't performing for Ringling Brothers and Barnum & Bailey in America under canvas or in the largest venues like Madison Square Garden, they performed in Europe during the winter. Newspapers here and abroad covered their touring schedule, as well as nearly every move they made outside the circus ring.

In 1931, Lillian Leitzel was scheduled to present her act in Copenhagen, while the Flying Codonas were scheduled to do so in Berlin's famed venue Wintergarten. The unimaginable rocked Copenhagen and, soon thereafter, the world: just as Lillian began her planges, the swivel on her ring shattered, sending her to the floor thirty feet below. She was rushed to a local hospital, and Alfredo was summoned. Reports vary on what happened next: either she regained consciousness and railed at Codona to leave her and honor his contract in Wintergarten, or her doctors assured him that she was well enough for him to return there, but on February 15, 1931, while he was on a train back to Berlin, Codona's beloved wife died.

Alfredo was devastated. Canceling his contract, he went back to Copenhagen. The great Leitzel was cremated, and a funeral service was held there. News of her death was broadcast widely in the press and particularly in America, where her star truly shined brightest. Nearly a year later, on December 10, 1931, Lillian's ashes were interred at Inglewood Park Cemetery in Inglewood, California. There, Alfredo erected a magnificent marble monument of himself as a winged angel carrying his love Lillian to heaven. At his statue's feet are two rings, one shattered.

A little more than a year after Lillian's death, Alfredo married Vera Bruce, an aerialist in his troupe, but his flying became increasingly reckless. While performing a triple somersault in 1933, he severely dislocated his shoulder. He took a few weeks off to recuperate while Bert Doss, a Bloomington leaper, briefly took his place in the act. Alfredo came back before the injury was properly healed, further damaging his muscle and ensuring he would never fly again. Consequently, he spiraled into the darkest abyss of depression. By 1937, Vera wanted out of their marriage. In the office where he met Vera to finalize their divorce, he asked the attorney to leave him to speak with his soon-to-be ex-wife and her mother. He took out a pistol and shot Vera five times and ended his own life with the sixth bullet.

Codona's shoulder injury left a tremendous void in the center ring of the world's largest circus. Bloomington's Concello troupe by this time had performed in some of the world's most prestigious venues, Cirque D'Hiver in Paris, the Scala and Wintergarten in Berlin and the Olympia in London among them. They were asked to fill the center ring position left vacant by the Codonas, and they did so with unparalleled success. By this time, Art was throwing the triple somersault, a trick that few could do and fewer still could do with consistency. It was the gold standard of flying trapeze tricks. An exchange between an interviewer, George Brinton Beal, and Concello documents the time and effort it took to master it:

> *Beal: You have had falls, of course. Tell me about that, if you don't mind.*
> *Concello: Oh yes, I have come down lots of times since I started flying. I came down 900 times when I was working on one trick. You have to learn to hit the net when the trick fails, that's all.*
> *Beal: I notice, Mr. Concello, that you say "come down" and not use the word "fall." Is there a particular reason for that?*
> *Concello: I don't know that there is, but we usually say it that way.*[109]

Perhaps most people would rest on their laurels after achieving center ring fame. Not so with the Concellos. Antoinette, still enchanted by the thrill and glamour of being a trapeze star, wanted more. She began training to do the triple somersault in the Ward barn that was purchased by her husband in 1935.[110] Asked to comment on "the Farm," as Concello called the building, he told an interviewer, "I bought Eddie Ward's barn out in my home town of Bloomington, Illinois, and merely went on with Eddie's work…I train the members of my various flying acts there during the winter season. I suppose you would call it a school. We have the apparatus set up there, and a net stretched, just as you see it at the Garden. The only difference is that there is a sort of cat-walk along one side from which I can watch and criticize the flyers."[111] Years later, he described the dimensions of it in a snarling tone that was every bit Caesar-like and therefore completely Art Concello: "That sunabitch is 100 feet by 60 feet and 45 feet high."[112]

When asked if his wife could do the triple in 1935, Art replied, "Yes, I think she'll get it all right in time. She is unusually quick, mentally and physically. Flying and somersaulting comes natural to her, and she has plenty of confidence."[113] Just like Art, she missed hundreds of them in pursuit of her goal. Eddie Ward Jr. was her catcher as she learned the trick. His words were forever seared into her mind about perfecting it "as a combined college yell, piece of advice and a prayer…the sound of her name, necessarily shortened as she whipped by for points [in the net] unknown: 'Watch it, Auntie!'"[114]

In 1937, she eventually caught the trick: "I did the triple successfully in public for the first time in Detroit. Eddie Stinson, manager of Detroit's Shrine Circus, gave me a new dress to remember the occasion. There were years of hard, wearing practice before I succeeded, but Detroit's our lucky

A lineup of Concello-managed aerialists in the Ringling Brothers and Barnum & Circus backyard, 1937. *Left to right*: Gracie Genders, LaVon Bornhauser, Harold "Tuffy" Genders, unknown, Art and Antoinette Concello, Eddie Ward Jr., Marian Bordner, Wayne Larey and Bob Porter.

city."[115] She again performed it in Sheboygan, Wisconsin,[116] and likely other cities later that year and probably also in a few successive years. Though she never caught the triple consistently, the fact that their troupe was the first to feature a male and female flyer who could do so at all ensured their stature as stars of the circus. Art described what it felt like being up there flying thirty feet or more over the heads of the spectators below: "Up there, so high in the air, with [the] band playing, there is a sort of freedom. Now, standing here on the solid floor before a microphone, it sounds sort of silly, but there is a kind of ecstasy in flying through the air...I like it."[117]

While Antoinette was visualizing her form midair and determining how to add new tricks, her husband was often scheming. While standing on the pedestal board, his mind didn't always focus on the audience, the weather or plans for dinner. Instead, ideas about increasing his bank account swirled through his mind as he smoked his nearly omnipresent cigar; Concello seemed to think best with a stogie in his mouth (he often consumed up to twenty of them in a day).[118] He and the people he managed always stayed busy. He explained, "There is really plenty to do all the time. We make all our own nets, and the girls make the costumes. On the road we have plenty of repairs to do. And we have to keep enough resin ready to use."[119] While high above the crowd, he developed the habit of counting the house, doing so with unnerving accuracy. In addition, he used his free time to think of ways of doing things faster and better. He wanted to be in management.

Concello adopted and expanded the successful act management technique his mentor and former manager, Eddie Ward, had developed. Ward hired individual athletes like Art, Antoinette and others and then assembled flying troupes to be booked. Concello's early managerial notes are documented in his 1931 diary, which first details in careful script on the front page his height, weight, hat, shoe and glove size—five feet four inches, 130 pounds, 7⅛", 5½ and 8, respectively. The pages near the back list the cost of supplying "2 fours & one 3 people" acts to circuses and then lists the performers in each act by name, if known, like this:

Tuffy:	*55.00*
Bob:	*35.00*
Gracie:	*30.00*
Elden:	*30.00*
Salarys [sic]	*150.00*
+ Rigging	*20.00*
Total Cost	*170.00*[120]

The expenses for this act and two others are recorded on the same page. The profit for each was calculated, and finally Concello's cut for the week was documented: $510. In today's dollars, that would be roughly $7,500. Not bad money for a weekly salary, likely even by Concello's standards. He was well on his way to becoming the world's top trainer and manager of flying trapeze acts. That year, he built and supplied a total of nine flying acts for circuses in the United States, England and Australia.[121]

Along with act management, Concello morphed into something bystanders might call a loan shark. The diary for 1934–35 initially reports performance details like "November 31, Paris France, Mat[inee] missed tripple [sic] nite [sic] okay." Toward the back of this gem, people's names are recorded along with how much money they owed to him. Payment schedules are also documented. At the back of this book is a "Memoranda and Addresses" section. The first few names recorded there demonstrate the depth of Bloomington's impact on him: A. Vasconcellos, his father; C.D. Curtis, the YMCA coach who taught him his first trapeze skills, a man said to be "the greatest influence on his life";[122] and Harold Ramage, the connection to the Keiser-Van Leer hardware store, where so much rigging could be economically obtained. The other six names recorded include well-connected circus fans and the circus chairman of Detroit's Shrine Temple, Ed Stinson.[123]

The 1938 Ringling-Barnum workers' strike in Scranton, Pennsylvania, provided Concello an opportunity to curry favor with John Ringling North, the Ringling Brothers and Barnum & Bailey Circus's new president. At the root of the conflict between the union and management was a divergence of interpretation of the negotiated five-year union contract signed the previous year by the American Federation of Actors' executive secretary, Ralph Whitehead. North argued that poor business along with increased operating expenses necessitated slashed employee wages and offered to share the financial statements that proved that. Whitehead countered by suggesting that the financial records should be audited by certified public accountants but until that happened, the show should operate at its original contract rate. During this difficult period, a group of 250 performers headed by Art Concello signed a petition of loyalty to their employers.[124] In the ensuing impasse, the Big Show, as the Ringling Brothers and Barnum & Bailey Circus was known, retreated to Sarasota to regroup. Days later, many of the performers were on the road again performing in Redfield, South Dakota, under the title the "Al G. Barnes and Sells-Floto Circus presents Ringling Brothers and Barnum &

Bailey Stupendous New Acts."[125] The Flying Concellos and the Fearless Flyers, both made up of Bloomington personnel, provided the trapeze talent for this show.

Also in 1938, Concello provided North the money he needed to back a performance bond.[126] North questioned everything during this trying time, including the literal horsepower needed to load and unload the show. Concello's reply to him reads like the matter-of-fact manager he would become:

> The damn army moves all these heavy ammunition wagons and everything else with Caterpillar tractors. We ought to think about getting some tractors, and see if you can't eliminate those horses; and when you close, you can set them tractors over there and say "sit there now until I want you again," and it ain't gonna cost you a nickel. You might have to fix them up a little or something, but it ain't gonna eat every day.[127]

As Art's income increased, so did his spending—though the latter never outpaced the former. His assets grew to be as diverse as the personalities surrounding him in the big top so that by "the ripe age of 29, all he has to show for 13 years on the 'swing bar'—besides several diamonds big enough to go skating on and a handful of corns—are three farms, an apartment house and a beer garden back in Bloomington."[128]

Concello flew with his act until 1942, when he took over as general manager for Ringling Brothers and Barnum & Bailey. Everything he had experienced to that point helped to prepare him for this role, including his long-ago membership in Bloomington High School's Manual Arts Club. That club's purpose was "to promote interest in the industrial arts, to elevate the intellectual and social conditions of its members, and to encourage a spirit of loyalty."[129] Concello could only satisfy his curiosity and ambition by learning as much about the Big Show as he could by being everywhere from the front office to the backyard, by listening and by learning everyone's names and responsibilities. He made himself useful throughout the 1930s so that by 1942, when he was asked to assume the general manager role of the Ringling Brothers and Barnum & Bailey Circus, "The Greatest Show on Earth," he stepped in with aplomb.

Eileen Voise sewing a costume in front of a circus wardrobe trunk. Date unknown.

CHAPTER 8

STAY FOR AS LONG AS YOU CAN FOR AS MUCH AS YOU CAN

THE RISE OF ART CONCELLO, MANAGER, OWNER, IMPRESARIO

The physical agility that a flyer required to successfully perform tricks in the air needed to be at least matched—if not doubled—by a mental agility to negotiate the logistical tricks required to keep a circus running smoothly. In 1942, Concello entered management, where he became one of the most highly regarded and innovative circus executives. He was that rare individual who started out as a world-class performer and then successfully transitioned into management. That he continued running the practice barn on Emerson Street in Bloomington and managing a slew of flying acts only added to his legend.

Just days into the Ringling Brothers and Barnum & Bailey 1942 season, George W. Smith, the general manager since 1938, was replaced, surprisingly, by the relatively untested Concello, who was already responsible for the three flying acts on the show at the time.[130] A major crisis sprang up that season, and it is painfully obvious to call this Concello's trial by fire, because that is exactly what it was. On August 4, 1942, in Cleveland, Ohio, Ringling's 320-by 120-foot six-pole menagerie tent burned to the ground, killing some forty to fifty animals in the blaze. Among the dead were four elephants, thirteen camels, nine zebras, two giraffes, four lions, two tigers, one llama, one puma, two brindled gnus, three Indian deer and two midget burros.[131] Though intrigue ran high, no clear cause of the fire became evident beyond the unfortunate waterproofing technique used for the tents: coating them with a ridiculously flammable mixture of paraffin and gasoline. It bears mentioning that during Ringling's infamous fire in Hartford, Connecticut, in July 1944 (Concello was no longer with the show), this waterproofing proved fatal to more than the animals, killing over 150 circus-goers and injuring hundreds more. The general manager at that time was, again, George W. Smith, who was arrested along with a number of other circus executives to answer for the deadly debacle. Despite the fire, Concello turned in a respectable job as a first-time general manager for 1942.

By January 1943, John Ringling North, president of the Ringling Brothers and Barnum & Bailey Circus, and Henry Ringling North, vice-president, lost control of the show to Robert Ringling, son of one of the original founders, Charles Ringling. As a result of this change, Concello was removed from his position as general manager, and the organization was once again run by George W. Smith. Concello still had a contract with the show to provide flying acts for that season.[132] The star aerial act for it that year was the Flying Concellos, consisting of Antoinette Concello, Eddie Ward Jr. and Dude Rhodus.[133]

Concello is more often associated with the Big Show, but from 1943 to 1947, he cut his teeth working angles as a shrewd businessman by becoming a circus owner. Hitting the ground running after his first departure from Ringling, Concello wasted no time building his already impressive résumé.

In June 1943, Concello—along with his partners, animal trainer Jack Joyce and concessionaire Lou Berg—purchased the Russell Brothers Circus from Claude and Pauline Russell Webb.[134] The Russell Brothers show at the time of purchase was a truck show, meaning that the circus traveled by trucks rather than by rail, as did larger shows like Ringling Brothers and Barnum & Bailey. By December 1943, the breakdown of this partnership came to light as both Joyce and Berg filed for dissolution of their agreement, citing friction with Concello. This issue seems to have come to a boiling point when Concello reportedly barred his partners from the lot while the circus had been in Denver the previous October. They also claimed that Concello had refused to address their queries about the earnings. Each man had put up money toward the $50,000 purchase price for the circus, and both Joyce and Berg sought to have their individual investments returned to them.[135] Concello and Joyce continued to work on the same show for the next few seasons, alluding to some sort of resolution between them.

With the 1944 season at hand, Concello joined with Clyde Beatty, the legendary animal trainer. Russell Brothers Circus was then rechristened as the Clyde Beatty and Russell Bros. Combined Circus. The Flying Concellos

Art Concello as general manager of Ringling Brothers and Barnum & Bailey Circus with Boss Canvasman Bill "Captain" Curtis, 1942.

were featured as the star aerial act consisting of Antoinette Concello, Gracie Genders, Elden Day and Joe Remillette. They were described in the route book and printed program for that season as "Absolutely Fearless Performers Who Scoff at the Laws of Gravity and Fly Through Space like Winged Birds." Antoinette also produced and performed with a large Spanish web display known as Ballet of the Sky. Concello's half sister Grace Killian was on the show as treasurer, a position Art had her take later with Ringling Brothers and Barnum & Bailey. Former Concello partner Jack Joyce and his wife, Martha, also had acts with the show—military ponies and liberty horses, respectively. Ed Raycraft, Bloomington's premier Cadillac and LaSalle automobile dealer and occasional benefactor of and friend to Art Concello, was also pressed into service with the show, working the front door.[136]

The Beatty-Concello partnership ended after the 1944 season. Concello's new show, this time called Russell Bros. Pan-Pacific Circus, took to the rails for the first time, incorporating equipment from the Beckman and Gerety Shows.[137] A few key managers from the Ringling show defected to work with Concello. The biggest score from the ranks of Ringling was undoubtedly Roland Butler, press agent, bill writer and iconic artist of so many of the memorable illustrations found on Ringling posters. The marvelous Cristiani Family of equestrians was on the bill, along with other first-rate talent like the Rink Wright Duo, Arthur Konyot and, of course, the Flying Concellos. Antoinette Concello, who gave birth to Randall Cope Concello on February 16, 1945, was featured on the show a few months later performing the daring two and a half somersault—meaning the catcher caught her by her feet rather than her hands. She wrote a brief article for the Russell Bros. Pan-Pacific Circus program detailing the gritty reality of what an aerialist faced, time and time again, while delighting thousands with feats of skill and grace:

> *Death or permanent disability always confronts us. I remember once, in August, in a small Iowa town, up above it was impossible to keep our hands dry. As I swung back and forth several times to gather momentum, I felt my hands gradually slipping from the bar. I realized I had to hurry or I would slip before leaving my trapeze for the somersault. Although I should have swung back and forth at least another three times—I let go and started the turns.*
>
> *Well, I managed to get over two-and-a-half times all right—but my feet were about four or five inches short of the catcher's hands—so that he got a very poor grip on me, and the next second I started to fall*

Aerialists in the 1949 season of Ringling Brothers and Barnum & Bailey Circus. *Left to right*: Dorothy Durbin, Antoinette Concello, Ann Robbins and Kay Clark.

> *There was an oval net under me but I fell into the apron. As I hit the apron, the rope pegs gave way and I fell again—about twenty feet.*
>
> *But our "helper," a strong young boy who takes care of the equipment, stepped right under me as I started my second fall—and caught me in his arms! I escaped unhurt.*
>
> *I would like to point out to the bloodthirsty ones that it is just as easy to be killed falling to the net as to a wooden platform. In fact, I have seen several people killed in net falls.*
>
> *Unless you fall to the net correctly—disaster or death is certain.*[138]

Famous comedian Milton Berle also wrote a brief article called "No Clowning..." in the same program.

Art Concello and Clyde Beatty again struck a deal to join forces for the 1946 season under the title of the Clyde Beatty Circus; gone was Russell Bros. Pan-Pacific. As a result of negotiations, Concello got a stake in Beatty's

Three circus greats colliding for a photo opportunity. *Left to right*: former equestrian and Shrine Circus producer Orrin Davenport and equestrian Corky Cristiani with Art Concello in 1947.

show; he owned the circus train; and the Flying Concellos were featured on the bill, this time consisting of Jeannie Sleeter, Elden Day, Joe Siegrist and Red Sleeter. Eventually, the train, the equipment and the stake in the show were sold to Beatty outright with the exception of Concello's private train car named for his only son, "The Randy."[139] The Flying Concellos continued on the bill for the Clyde Beatty Circus during the 1947 season.

RETURN TO RINGLING

John Ringling North regained control of Ringling Brothers and Barnum & Bailey Circus in November 1947. With North's return, it was announced that Art Concello would step back into the role of general manager of the circus,[140] replacing, once again, George W. Smith, who eventually took the position of manager for the Dailey Bros. Circus in 1948.[141] John Ringling North's fortunate turn with the Ringling show was made possible with the shrewd help of a loan of $100,000 from Concello, who, it is said, borrowed a portion of it from his friend and occasional financier from Bloomington, Ed Raycraft.[142]

The 1948 season was a watershed for innovations that streamlined the operation of the circus. The big game changer was the revolutionary seat wagon designed by Concello and Lester Thomas,[143] a former aerialist who had flown alongside Concello in their early days with the Flying Wards. The hydraulically erected and interlocking tubular steel grandstand wagons took the place of the labor-intensive and train-hogging steel and wood bleachers that typically took 250 men over two hours to set up, while Concello's design required one hour's work and only 14 men. Not only did the seating take less time to erect, dismantle and move, but more importantly to the patron of the circus, it was actually comfortable, thanks to the rubber cushions and individual seatbacks. Another Concello innovation was changing the structure of the animal arenas used in the performance from its original 3,500-pound and twenty-five-section steel construction to the light and space-saving nickel chain steel mesh that weighed a mere fraction of the former construction and moved on a single wagon.[144] At the same time, Concello set the groundwork to eventually replace the wooden quarterpoles of the big top with thinner, less obtrusive aluminum poles. When all was said and done, these thoughtful and innovative designs cut down the number of rail cars needed to move the Big Show—from 108 cars to a lean 70.[145]

Antoinette Concello returned to the flying trapeze in 1949 for Ringling-Barnum after a yearlong absence due to a shoulder injury, an occupational hazard common to aerial performers. Though she was no longer catching big tricks, her showmanship and styling were still impeccable.

Cecil B. DeMille, the legendary director, began work on *The Greatest Show on Earth* in March 1950 with cooperation from the Ringling Bros. and Barnum & Bailey Circus. The film, which packs in just about every possible emotional turn, stars Charlton Heston in the role of Brad Braden, the tough-talking, pragmatic show boss. It is said that the character was modeled, in part, after Bloomington and Ringling's very own "Little Caesar" himself, Art Concello. Antoinette Concello, Harold "Tuffy" Genders and other familiar Bloomingtonians with the circus also made brief on-screen cameos in the film.

Concello again left Ringling Bros. and Barnum & Bailey Circus in December 1953 after a disagreement with John Ringling North about the size of the circus. Concello wanted to trim it down to fifty rail cars, but North intended to do nothing of the sort. He did not want to truncate the show one bit, insisting that if the circus were to run aground, it would do so

One of Art Concello's patented seat wagons being offloaded from the Ringling train in 1952.

in the grandeur befitting it.[146] Another source of upheaval for the Concellos was that in 1953, Antoinette Concello retired from flying.

In this particular time away from the Ringling show, Concello purchased the controlling interest in the problematic Clyde Beatty Circus in January 1955[147] only to flip it back to Clyde Beatty by 1956. Art held a chattel mortgage on the show that was eventually foreclosed on due to the show running into an unfixable tangle of trouble that included bad weather, slow business and a walkout by the show's unionized performers for unpaid wages,[148] leading it to be quartered early. A judgment in favor of Concello in excess of $57,000 was handed down, leading to an auction of all the Clyde Beatty Circus property at the Luna County Courthouse in Deming, New Mexico, in the summer of 1956.[149]

That year, 1956, was a season of lasts. It marked the final year Art and Antoinette traveled together as man and wife, their divorce being finalized in September. It was also the last season under canvas for the Ringling Bros. and Barnum & Bailey Circus, and it was a troubled one at that, stopping midway through with its future looking particularly grim. Concello was called back into the fold one more time to successfully retool the show in order to play in arenas. He did so by using his knack for bold practicality combined with cost cutting, as he had done before. Shrine circuses had been playing arenas for decades by the time Ringling made the change to play inside buildings instead of under canvas. The show left winter quarters for the 1957 season sans tent and train (although the train came back by 1960)[150] to play both indoor and some outdoor venues.

Another Ringling-sized headache came for Concello in February 1958. It became known as the "49ers" issue, and it was complicated. Jerry Collins, of the Clyde Beatty Circus, offered to buy the Ringling show outright. Minority shareholders in the show, calling themselves the "49ers," were led by Stuart Lancaster, the grandson of Charles Ringling. They mobilized an aggressive opposition of the sale. Concello was served with papers in a mismanagement lawsuit brought by the 49ers that sought to oust Ringling management and $20 million in damages. While rumblings of 49er discontent with the North-Concello team had been known since midway through the 1957 season,[151] the 49ers met with little legal support, and a number of the motions that they brought forward to halt any potential sale of the circus as a whole or in part were denied. By the end of February 1958, the Ringling Brothers and Barnum & Bailey Circus, as a name or intellectual property, was officially not for sale, but the show's animals, equipment and train were.[152] A few short years of heavy bluster resulted in nothing, however. All the suits filed by the 49ers were dropped or dismissed by June 1960, and the show, indeed, continued to go on.[153] Despite all the legal trouble, the Big Show thrived financially beyond its tented days. Concello was back and forth with the show in the years that followed. Regardless of who he was working with or for, Art was always working an angle and, more often than not, was hugely successful in his business ventures.

Art Concello working an angle as general manager of Ringling Brothers and Barnum & Bailey Circus, circa 1949. Merely eight years prior, he had been one of the star aerialists.

Antoinette Concello continued her career with Ringling for decades as aerial director and was known to step in and up for other aerialists in their absence, doing so with the same grace and astonishing athleticism that made her world acclaimed for so many years. She was inducted in Peru, Indiana's Circus Hall of Fame in 1963. She stayed with Ringling until shortly before her death in February 1984, when she succumbed to lung cancer. Antoinette is buried in Bloomington, Illinois' Park Hill Cemetery (her headstone erroneously spells her name Antonilette), in the Comeau family plot alongside her parents and siblings, including her sister Gertrude "Mickey" King, a famous aerialist in her own right.

Art Concello married Maggie Smith in Florida in July 1984. Maggie, a lovely English blonde, had been with the Ringling show as a member of the Wallabies and in the aerial ballet. Art and Maggie had long been together as a couple.

Concello died in Sarasota in July 2001. Though he had been involved in countless business dealings in his long career, it was his time managing Ringling Brothers and Barnum & Bailey Circus that best underlines what made him managerially great. He was a logistical and fiscal savant of the highest order, born under the right sign, landing on his feet nearly every time. He was crucial to the show at pivotal points in its history and was able to maintain its relevancy in an era full of competition for the public's dollars and time.

THE SNEEZE MOB

Throughout Concello's tenure on shows, two things were constants: his tenacity and the Sneeze Mob. Trusted individuals were placed in positions of authority, and as a sideline, for some, they would run graft operations on the show, kicking back a set percentage of whatever ill-gotten gains to Concello (or, in the case of Ringling Brothers and Barnum & Bailey, whomever was in charge in Concello's absence) for the privilege. These rackets took the form of illegal gambling, booze, duplicate ticket schemes and all other manner of cons that would wire the show in the favor of the workingmen to compensate for the low wages on the circus lot.[154] Beyond this basic description of the Sneeze Mob, rumors and speculation run amok. Concello didn't invent the Sneeze Mob, but he benefited from it both financially and in the way that it smoothed out aspects of operating the show. It has its detractors and its defenders, but one thing is for certain: the real specifics of it remain elusive.

Tony Steele receives a well-deserved pat on the back from Art Concello as husband and wife June and Mike Malko bask in the moment for this publicity still for the Flying Malkos.

Chapter 9
A Consortium of Curious Characters

Bloomington was, and to many throughout the world still is, synonymous with the craft of the trapeze. Though it was not invented here, the city once teemed with eager students of the aerial arts, more so than any other place on the planet. This chapter captures a fraction of the people and the acts that called Bloomington home, either by birth or as a kind of Mecca for breaking into show business by way of a swinging silver bar.

Flying Arbaughs

The Flying Arbaughs consisted of the husband-and-wife team of seasoned Bloomington flyers Jim Arbaugh and Jessie. The couple had been members of the Flying Wards before they formed their own flying return act. Jessie Arbaugh was born Jessie Hubbell. Her sister Mabel Hubbell was a Flying Ward and later wife of famed Hollywood movie cowboy and circus owner Tom Mix. Erma Hubbell, another sister, was also with the Wards and known for her one-arm plange or muscle grind. The Flying Arbaughs regularly played parks and fairs as well as circuses.

The Flying Arbaughs (the Arbaugh Family) as they were featured on a 1937 Tom Mix Circus poster.

FLYING ARTONYS

The Flying Artonys was an example of a Concello-managed act. It included Billy Ward, Red and Mitzi Sleeter, Bones Brown, Walter Graybeal, Jeannie Sleeter, Jimmy Crocker and Harold and Gracie Genders in the act at different times. The troupe shared its name with Art Concello's holding company, Artony, a combination of "Art" and "Tony" (Antoinette's nickname). The troupe worked Shrine dates, fairs and circuses from Al G. Barnes & Sells-Floto Circus to Ringling Brothers and Barnum & Bailey Circus on and off from the late 1930s to the early 1950s. The Flying Artonys appeared alongside the Flying Concellos and the Flying Comets in Cecil B. DeMille's Academy Award–winning film *The Greatest Show on Earth* in 1952 while on Ringling.

FLYING BRONTES

The Flying Brontes was one of Concello's flying acts and may have only existed for the 1948 season with Ringling Brothers and Barnum & Bailey Circus alongside the Artonys and the Flying Comets. The troupe consisted of Willie Krause, Jeannie Sleeter, Bones Brown and Jimmy Crocker.

FLYING COMETS/FLYING COVETS

The Flying Comets or, alternately, the Flying Covets was another of the many flying return acts in Concello's stable of top-quality talent. The act performed in all manner of venues, from high-profile Ringling spots to Shrine dates and fairs. While the lineup of the troupe frequently changed, former Flying Ward flyer Wayne Larey, known for his prowess with the triple somersault, and catcher Bob Porter were mainstays. Other notable members of the Flying Comets include Jeannie Sleeter, daughter of aerialists Red and Mitzi Sleeter (and niece to Gracie and Harold "Tuffy" Genders); Carl "China" Durbin and his wife, Dorothy; Everett White; and Mike Kocuik, who would later form the Flying Malkos. Wayne Larey was married at one time to flyer Eileen Sullivan, daughter of circus veteran James "Soda" Sullivan. Wayne and Eileen divorced, and she later married fellow aerialist Harold Voise.

As the Flying Covets, Larey led the troupe to Australia, where it performed successfully throughout the 1940s with the popular Wirth Circus and others. Larey enjoyed a long career in the circus and later produced them around the globe in places such as South America, Russia and throughout Europe.

The Flying Comets began trouping in 1937 with Tuffy and Gracie Genders as the leapers of the act. The troupe also appeared in the film *The Greatest Show on Earth*.

BERT AND AGNES DOSS

Delbert Doss was born in Piqua, Ohio, in 1903 but moved with his family as a child to Bloomington. Delbert, who often went by the name Bert, struck up a friendship with Eddie Ward of the Flying Wards at the very time that he was building what would become the legendary practice barn at 1201 East Emerson Street in 1915. Later in life, Bert recounted to the *Daily Pantagraph* that he helped carry wood during the construction of the barn, and in return, Ward let him jump around in the safety net. Bert was eventually brought into the Wards as a clown, but shortly thereafter, Eddie broke in Bert as a flyer.

In his professional travels with the Flying Wards, Bert met fellow aerialist Agnes Marine. Born in Edgewater, Colorado, in 1907, Agnes's interest in the circus started in childhood while living in Denver near the winter quarters of the popular Sells-Floto Circus, which she passed on her way to and from school, often stopping to watch the performers rehearsing. The magic in the winter quarters fascinated her.[155] She later performed with her sisters Ethyl and Neva in an aerial act called the D'Arcy Girls.

Bert and Agnes married in Bloomington in 1927. After their time with the Flying Wards, the couple continued on with a number of other troupes, including the Flying Thrillers (made up at different times by Harold Voise, Bob Brooks, Bert Doss, Red and Mitzi Sleeter and Frank Shepard) and the Flying Bertons (with a lineup of Bert and Agnes Doss and Eddie Ward Jr.). Agnes Doss was particularly known for her solo act performing aerial web and single trapeze feats, especially one-arm planges.

Early in the 1933 season, Alfredo Codona of the world-famous Flying Codonas suffered a career-ending shoulder injury while the troupe was part of Ringling Brothers and Barnum & Bailey Circus. Bert Doss was pressed into service as his temporary replacement (Doss was later replaced by Clayton Behee). The Flying Thrillers were a featured act in 1934 for a three-month engagement with the Chicago World's Fair Century of Progress International Exposition at the Lagoon Theatre.

After Bert and Agnes retired from performance, they opened a roller-skating rink called Circus Park Rink on land that is now the G.J. Mecherle Memorial Park (State Farm Park) in the southern part of Bloomington. Their business later moved to 107 East Lafayette Street, now the Lafayette Club (formerly the Tiara Ballroom), where it was called the Circus Roller Rink.

The Dosses had two children, Ethyl and Jeanice, born in 1928 and 1939, respectively. Tragically, Ethyl died in her bed in 1944 at the age of sixteen from a gunshot wound. Jeanice died in 1988.

Agnes Doss died of leukemia in 1960. Bert remarried a local by the name of Ruth Barr in 1963 and died in 1970. Bert and Agnes are interred together in Park Hill Cemetery in Bloomington.

Left to right: Lalo Codona, Vera Bruce and Bert Doss. Bert Doss stands in for injured trapeze superstar Alfredo Codona in the Flying Codonas.

Agnes Doss in a posed publicity image displaying her undeniable glamour.

Gene and Mary Enos

This husband-and-wife team was known for its prowess on the rolling globe, as well as a phenomenal perch pole act with the atypical distinction of Mary working as her husband's "understander." Their act is described during their time with the Downie Bros. Circus in 1928 as "Gene and Mary Enos, the last word in head to head and perch pole balancing act, in which this sturdy little lady Mary supports and balances a pole of twenty-five feet while Gene performs various capers on the very top."[156]

In 1918, Gene and Mary were on the Hagenbeck-Wallace show (as were the Flying Wards), where they were involved in a horrific train wreck near Hammond, Indiana. The fiery collision of a speeding, empty U.S. Army troop transport train and the stationary circus train injured or killed over two hundred employees and performers of that circus. As a testament to Mary's sturdiness, after being rescued from the wreckage of the accident by firefighters, she rushed back into a smoldering car to search for Gene.[157] Mary later emerged from the destroyed train dragging her unconscious husband.[158]

The Enoses later furnished equipment from their act for use in Illinois State Normal University's Gamma Phi Circus.

Flying Flemings

Herb and Rose Fleming, like many alums of the Flying Wards, formed their own act. Herb Fleming was born in Decatur, Illinois, in 1896. Rose was born Rose Maurek in 1894. Herb broke into flying with Harry La Van of the Flying La Vans and later found a spot in the Flying Fishers before working with the Flying Wards.

The Flying Flemings worked through the better part of the 1930s, starting with the Hagenbeck-Wallace Circus in 1930 with a lineup consisting of couples Herb and Rose Fleming and Paul and Nellie Sullivan (of the Flying Sullivans), and later filled countless dates working vaudeville, parks and fairs across the country. A press notice described an enlarged version of their act in 1935: "Three girls, three boys, two acts. Double somersaults while blindfolded; double twists forward and backward, and many other feats. Miss Enid, a youthful aerialist of prodigious skill, introducing her original cloud swing."[159]

Rose Fleming, along with Evelyn Simpson and Madge Dayton, also had an act called the Fleming Sisters, in which they performed iron jaw, cloud swing, muscle grinds and single trapeze.[160] Rose worked in 1936 with the Flying LeClairs alongside Clarence "Kank" Croutcher and Pierre "Frenchy" La Framboise. Herb Fleming died in 1938 at the age of forty-two of what

The Flying Flemings. *Left to right*: Rose Fleming, Elmo Rankin, Evelyn Fleming, Elden Day, Madge Dayton and Herb Fleming.

is believed to be a heart attack. Rose later married Cole Brothers Circus bandleader Eddie Woeckener in 1945 but met a terrible end in 1946 while living on the outskirts of Peru, Indiana. Rose and Eddie tried to put out a grass fire on their property, but Rose perished after getting tangled in a wire fence.[161] Both Herb and Rose (under the married name of Woeckener) are interred in Park Hill Cemetery.

FLYING HAROLDS

The Flying Harolds was Harold Voise's flying return act that ran from the 1930s to the mid-1950s. It had an extensive list of associated performers including Harold Voise; Jack Voise; Eileen Voise (the former Eileen Larey); Harold "Tuffy" Genders and his wife, Gracie; Roy Deisler and his wife, Jaunita; Jean Evans; Elden Day; Dick Anderson; Bob Porter; Jack Harris;

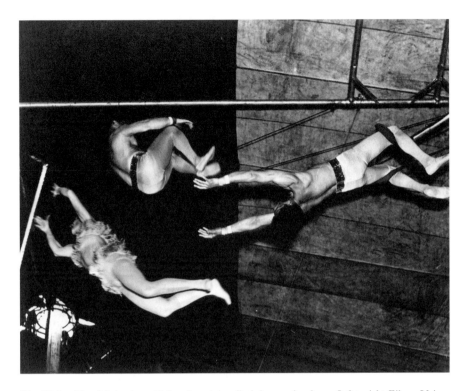

The Flying Harolds in the middle of a trick called the passing leap. *Left to right*: Eileen Voise, Harold Voise and Jack Voise.

Harold Harris; Christine Johnson; Ann Russell; and Rose Sullivan Behee. In 1953, the Flying Harolds performed their act in the MGM film *The Story of the Three Loves*, directed by Vincente Minelli.[162] Harold Voise went on to become a successful producer of his own shows under the moniker of Harold Bros. Circus and would often contract for Shrine dates throughout the country.

RAY HENDRYX

Ray Hendryx was born in Bloomington in 1899[163] and began performing with Gene and Mary Enos at the age of twelve on the rolling globe. He worked in a number of popular flying acts, among them the Flying Wards, the La Vans, the Flying Charles Siegrist Troupe and Bob Fisher's

Fearless Flyers. He also worked with Harry La Mar. Hendryx was injured in a trapeze accident in 1935, ending his career in show business. At age forty-one, Hendryx inexplicably fell over the railing of a passenger train just south of Jolliet, Illinois, while traveling with his friend John Penn, who had an appointment at a VA hospital there. Hendryx was killed, his friend's suitcase clutched in his hand as he fell from the train. This fact led to Penn's initial reluctance to report the incident for fear of being arrested.

WILLIAM F. "HAPPY" HUNT AND THE TILDEN-HALL HOTEL

"Happy" Hunt was the much-beloved manager of the Hotel Tilden Hall in Bloomington, which was located downtown at 219 West Washington Street (the corner of Washington and Madison Streets, now a parking lot). Hotel Tilden Hall, because of Hunt's charm and easy friendship with local circus folk, became a second home to show people from all over the world, many of whom came to town to practice at the Ward/Concello barn and/ or at the YMCA. For many years, an annual dinner was held at the hotel to celebrate Hunt's friendship with circus folk.[164]

FLYING (AKA AERIAL, IMPERIAL, PEERLESS) ILLINGTONS

This flying return act was likely named in homage to Bloomington-born Broadway stage and silent screen actress Margaret Illington. The Illingtons at one time consisted of the husband-and-wife team Billy and Virginia Ward and Carl Lasater and regularly played circuses, parks and fairs. Carl Lasater died on December 15, 1941, while his troupe was playing with the E.K. Fernandez Circus in Honolulu. He was awaiting a surgical procedure in the aftermath of the Pearl Harbor bombing.

Happy Hunt's birthday dinner at Bloomington's Tilden-Hall Hotel, January 16, 1947. *Back row*: Elden Day, Harold "Tuffy" Genders and Bill Warner. *Middle row*: Harold Ramage and Joe Siegrist. *Front row*: Art Vasconcellos Sr., Tom Salmon, Ginger Kohl, Milonge Escalante, Joan Siegrist Day, Mayme Ward, Jeannie Sleeter, Ala Ming and Eddie Kohl. Happy Hunt is seated in front.

MICKEY KING

Born Gertrude Comeau in 1905 to Toussaint and Jane Comeau in Sutton, Quebec, Canada, she was best known by her professional name, Mickey King. She was the sister of Antoinette Concello, the first woman to complete a triple somersault to the hands of a catcher. Mickey had been a member of the Flying Wards. During her tenure with them, she lived in the hallowed house that would in later years be called the Grand Hotel at 1201 East Emerson Street. Mickey's glamorous and alluring lifestyle as an aerialist was the reason that her younger sister, fresh from a convent school, didn't return to a life of quiet spiritual meditation. Both sisters were at one point members of the Flying Wards, along with Art Concello, who later married Antoinette.

Mickey's signature solo act consisted of aerial contortions on rings placed high above the ground, similar to that of the legendary Lillian Leitzel. Her

Aerialist Mickey King looking every bit the circus celebrity in her autographed publicity photograph that is affectionately inscribed to Harold Ramage. Ramage worked at Bloomington's hardware store, the Keiser-Van Leer Company, and often provided equipment needed to rig at an economical price.

prowess for the physically excruciating yet visually exhilarating one-arm plange, or muscle grind, is what won her the most accolades. Besides her solo act, Mickey was associated with a number of other aerial acts like the Flying Valentinos and the Flying DuWards, with whom she worked on and off throughout the mid-1940s. She played fairs and Shrine circus dates with Billy Ward and Carl and Dorothy Durbin.[165] In the early 1950s, she had an act with Billy Ward known as the Flying Kings.[166] Her skill, artistry and charisma took her all over the world. She was featured on the cover of *Billboard* magazine on November 2, 1935, as "Mickey King Internationally Renowned Aerialist" and was the recipient of that publication's first Aerial Women's Lillian Leitzel Memorial Medal in 1939.[167]

Mickey first married circus animal trainer Allen King in 1924 but later married circus performer Jimmy McLeod. Mickey King died in 2004 and is interred in the Comeau family plot in Bloomington's Park Hill Cemetery.

Aerial Lafayettes

Bert (James) McGinty and Jack Ernst, Bloomington youths, went on the road as the (Flying) Ernstonians with the Gollmar Brothers Circus during the 1909 season. By 1910, their partnership had dissolved. Their parting was fortuitous, at least at first, for both. McGinty went with the Aerial Lafayettes, while Ernst built the Ernstonians. Ernst found vaudeville and later international success with his act, earning a spot on the Wirth Circus in Australia and New Zealand as a four-person (two men and two women) aerial act. The Aerial Lafayettes began with Edward Lambke and Bert McGinty (who took the professional name of Bert Lafayette) but later featured only McGinty and his younger sister, Agnes. Their act was described in 1914 as "Sensational Double Trapeze Artists. An extraordinary act of power, skill and strength. Suspended by teeth or toes, they operate 40 feet above the earth without net or protection. It is a novel and brilliant act, full of dash, vigor and daring."[168]

Though more could be written about Bert's start in Bloomington as an aerial wunderkind, it's his ending that is so jarring. After achieving recognition as a popular act in vaudeville in the 1910s and earning a stint with Ringling Brothers, the Aerial Lafayettes were not hired back with the show. A letter from McGinty inquiring about placement on Ringling for 1917 was met with a sobering reply from Charles Ringling:

I believe we have been patient with you and that we tried to make it possible to keep you with the Ringling show. Personally I had hoped that you would consult your best interests and in a manly manner do that which was best for your health and wellfare [sic]. If you see it the way I do you will feel that you have made serious errors and if you see it further as I do this must not discourage you as you will profit by the experience of the past and take hold and do what you ought to now in [a] manly way. I certainly hope you will do this.[169]

Bert died in Oak Forest, Illinois, on April 29, 1917. The previous season, his sister Agnes had married Charles Thorton, a candy butcher, while on Ringling.[170] She was briefly attached to the Aerial Macks on the show, but it seems she didn't continue with circus life much longer without her brother.

During their short time of circus celebrity, the Aerial Lafayettes feuded with Bert's former partner, Edward Lambke, over the Lafayette moniker, and to that end, Lambke had his own competing act known as the Flying Lafayettes.

FLYING LA MARS

The Flying La Mars started with Edward Foreman, who performed as Ed La Mar in the later part of the nineteenth century and then worked with the Flying Fishers. La Mar later trained his nephew Harry Foreman, who became Harry La Mar, a key figure in Bloomington trapeze history because he was known to have trained so many young hopeful trapeze performers (Tony Steele among them). Like Eddie Ward and Art Concello, Harry produced finished, professional flyers and, through the Flying La Mars, continued his uncle's work well into the 1960s, placing acts with circuses, vaudeville, parks and fairs all over the world.

The *Manitoba Free Press* described the act in 1915: "The Flying La Mars, appearing at the Strand this week, are finished circus performers, they using a trapeze for their work. At intervals during their act they both fly out well over the heads of the audience and a single slip would mean instant death."[171]

The Flying La Mars. *Left to right*: Ray Hendryx, Velma Harvey, Hank Robbins, Betty Phillips and Harry Foreman (La Mar).

FLYING MALKOS/THE MALKO TROUPE

The Flying Malkos' name results from a combination of the last names of the founding members and married couple June Malcolm and Mike Kocuik, who headquartered in Bloomington throughout the 1950s. Kocuik, a one-time member of the Flying Comets, was the catcher. The troupe is most noted for its young member, flyer Tony Steele, who in 1962 made circus history (and an entry in *The Guinness Book of Records*) with the Flying Marilees by achieving the first three and a half somersault to a catcher. Tony Steele added the difficult triple somersault to his repertoire, however, while working with the Flying Malkos.

ULLAINE MALLOY

Ullaine Malloy was often described as the "blonde bombshell" of circus, and that title was not in any way undeserved. Born in Idaho in 1911, Malloy would later be known to Bloomingtonians as an attractive staple of the much acclaimed YMCA Circus. She was famous for her one-arm planges, or muscle grinds, and aerial ring contortions. Her career lasted from the 1930s into the 1950s, performing as a single attraction or, in rare occasions, as a part of a troupe.

The "Blonde Bombshell" Ullaine Malloy performing an aerial contortion at Bloomington's 1936 YMCA Circus.

ART MONETTE

Born John Arthur Anderson, the successful clown worked professionally as Art Monette, but he initially trained and performed as an aerialist. His early trapeze training was by his friend and fellow Bloomingtonian Bert McGinty

Charles Smith (left) of the Aerial Smiths and Art Monette of the Art Monette Trio pose here as their clown alter egos.

(Bert Lafayette), of whom he writes in his scrapbook, "My teacher Bert and Aggie McGinty—The Aerial Lafayettes The Greatest Double Trap Act of Them All—Apology To E. Ward and Chas. Smith."[172] This was high praise, considering that both Ward and Smith were quite famous by that time.

Over the course of Monette's nearly twenty-year career, he was a veritable jack-of-all-trades performance-wise. By his account he was a clown acrobat, aerialist, horseman, bump and stunt man, producing clown, mule rider, pigeon trainer, comedy musician and the paid personal bodyguard of "Buffalo Bill" himself, Colonel William Cody, on the Sells-Floto Circus.

FLYING SENSATIONS

This flying return act of M. Paul Thorpe, Wayne Bowers and Victor Gismundo is most notable for including Flying Ward alum Bee Starr. Starr's life outside of flying was especially interesting because she sued the Heavyweight Boxing Champion of the World, Max Baer, in what was termed a "heart balm" suit (unfulfilled or rescinded promise of marriage), asking for $150,000. Baer countersued for the same amount, as he claimed that such a charge was damaging to his good name.[173] Baer, it seems, was dogged by a number of these jilted-affairs-of-the-heart legal cases. Neither party won.

AERIAL SMITHS

The Aerial Smiths were a husband-and-wife act that was most popular at the turn of the twentieth century. They performed feats not unlike those of the early Flying Wards, but the Smiths, who predated them by a few years, had made it to the Big Show first, working many seasons with Ringling Brothers throughout that first decade of the century.

Charles (often called Charlie) and Ada Smith's act consisted of a double trapeze, one above the other, and featured tricks that included a variation of the then-ubiquitous iron jaw, in which Ada hung high above the tanbark from a leather strap clenched in her teeth. This strap was held aloft by her husband, who had the other end of it clenched in his teeth while he swung by his knees from the bar above him. The Aerial Smiths performed the audacious foot-to-foot catch that later became a highlight during the first few years of the Flying Wards' act. Charlie was also an accomplished clown who often pulled double duty by clowning and working the aerial act in the same show.

The Aerial Smiths worked tirelessly for a number of years as a popular vaudeville and circus act. They also found a great deal of success internationally, touring both Europe and Australia. Home was Bloomington, though, where Charlie often assisted with the clowning for the YMCA Circuses.

Charles and Ada Smith divorced, but the act continued with new female counterparts throughout the 1920s.

FLYING SULLIVANS

The Flying Sullivans was a flying return act featuring husband-and-wife Paul and Nellie Sullivan. Paul was born in Kentucky in 1890 but grew up in Bloomington. Before Paul's involvement with the trapeze, he married a local girl by the name of Jennie Fern Campbell, only to divorce her after less than a decade and a few hardships later. In 1919, Paul married Nellie, an English woman ten years his junior. Like many Bloomington flyers of a particular generation, the Sullivans had passed through the ranks of the Flying Wards, later to form their own troupe. A 1927 advertisement described the act: "High up in the air these daring aerialists fly through mid-air from one to another, now a series of somersaults, now a twisting revolution that is the limit of sensationalism. Not the least amazing is the lady member of this talented trio, whose startling feats start where the average male artist leaves off."[174]

The Flying Sullivans featured one and a half somersaults, half twisting doubles, double cutaways and a one-handed somersault to the catcher. Workhorse catcher George Valentine, later of the Flying Concellos and Flying Valentinos, caught for the act at one time. The Sullivans also worked with fellow Flying Wards alums Herb and Rose Fleming in the Flying Flemings.

Nellie Sullivan died in 1957. Paul Sullivan died in Florida in 1963.

THE FLYING VALENTINOS/FLYING VALENTINES/ FLYING ROMAS/FLYING LAVALS

The Valentine brothers of Bloomington-Normal—George, Fred, Roy and William—are a fascinating example of the lure of the trapeze, because each one developed his own act. George was the eldest of the Valentine brothers, born in 1898 in Bloomington. He was the first of the siblings to learn the art of flying at the local YMCA from the tireless Harry La Mar. George later worked with a number of notable acts, the Flying Sullivans and the Flying La Mars among them, and instructed his younger brothers in trapeze. Considered a consummate catcher, he was highly sought for flying return acts. George Valentine was the first catcher in the legendary Flying Concellos with husband-and-wife flyers Art and Antoinette Concello through their first season on Ringling Brothers and Barnum & Bailey Circus in 1931.

After leaving the Flying Concellos, George planned to form and manage his own act. Shortly thereafter, in 1932, he put together the Flying Valentinos with his Bloomington-born and -raised wife, Lorraine Mather Valentine, and champion speed skater and swimmer Geraldine "Sue" Pelto from Minnesota. Opting to join up with fairs and Shrine dates over the hustle and bustle of one-night-stand circuses, the Flying Valentinos made a name for themselves as a top-notch flying return act. The act was distinctive for featuring only female flyers. The Valentinos performed a full complement of daring aerial feats, often culminating with Lorraine Valentine's signature two and a half somersault while wearing a gunnysack over her head.

In 1948, George Valentine purchased the Happy Acres stables and several acres of surrounding property from William Caudell Sr. He hoped the property would become another training venue for acts of all kinds in the area. Valentine intended the facility, which is still standing, to be called Circus Haven. It is located on Grove Street in Normal and is currently owned by Illinois State University. While Valentine used this practice space, its ceiling was too low to practice a flying return act. The stables within it could not be removed for structural reasons.[175]

The Flying Valentinos transformed into a double trapeze act with Lorraine Valentine and Sue Pelto around 1950 when George Valentine

The Flying Valentinos perform outdoors, circa 1939. *Left to right*: George Valentine, Lorraine Valentine and Sue Pelto.

retired due to a heart condition. He died of a heart attack in 1955. The Valentino Sisters act continued until 1958. George and Lorraine had one child, Cherie, who, with the advantage of her parents' expert training, performed aerial acts in her youth and went on to appear on circuses for a number of years. Lorraine Valentine's retirement from performing eventually led her to work for State Farm Insurance, another notable Bloomington original. Lorraine died in 1987. Both she and George are interred in Park Hill Cemetery. Sue Pelto worked for Bloomington's Eureka Williams plant and then was employed as a building service worker for Illinois State University. Sue died in Florida in 1995.

Fred Valentine's flying return act, the Flying Valentines, at one time consisted of his brothers Roy and William, Hank Robbins, Jeep Milan and Lowell Scherer.

Roy "Runt" Valentine's flying return act was known as the Flying Romas with his wife, Mary Atterbury Valentine, who later went on to marry catcher Lee Stath, who famously caught Tony Steele's world-record three and a half somersault in 1962. The Flying Romas also included Jeep Milan and Mike Kocuik, later of the Flying Malkos.

William Valentine's flying return act was known as the Flying LaVals and appeared for many years in parks, fairs and Shrine circuses.

CHAPTER 10

The Last Chapter Is Not the End

The Fate of the Ward/Concello Practice Barn and the Grand Hotel

After the death of Eddie Ward in 1929, the Ward practice barn and associated property remained in use, with a rental fee paid by those practicing there, going toward the outstanding mortgage. This setup only lasted until August 1935, when Art Concello purchased the property. Use of the practice barn was then mostly restricted to Concello's acts.

By late 1939, plans were announced that would have changed Bloomington's role in the world of circus performers had they come to fruition. The *Daily Pantagraph* reported that Clyde Noble, formerly of the Flying Fishers and then a local jeweler, had proposed building a new training barn specifically to attract more performers to the area. The structure, costing an estimated $7,500 to $10,000, would have been bigger than the original Ward/Concello barn with dimensions of 60 by 120 feet with a 50-foot roof. The plan had a number of influential local backers, including Charles Hall, Clay Dooley, Clair McElhony and Henry Berenz. The hope was that such a facility would have enough business that it would be self-sustaining and revitalize the city's link to aerialists and that, with enough momentum, the facility would allow for expansion into other kinds of acts, specifically those using animals.[176] Unfortunately for Bloomington, none of it happened.

Clyde Noble, formerly of the Flying Fishers, places a wreath on the grave of Eddie and Jennie Ward in the 1950s.

By the 1950s, the Ward-Concello practice barn was well on its way toward disrepair. For a time, it was used as a storage facility. By late 1965, with the building all but dilapidated, thoughts turned to demolishing the iconic structure. *Daily Pantagraph* staff writer Dick Streckfuss described the facility as it stood derelict, awaiting its fate:

> *Well, it still stands, a ramshackle structure, towering higher than an ordinary barn has a right to do. Inside there's a sense of space and vacancy, a vacancy accentuated here and there by bundles of debris. Light comes from windows set high in the walls, windows which were meant to serve fliers, not groundlings. Mice rustle between the walls. A hole-riddled poster of the Concello flying act forms a partial wall for what must have been a dressing area. In the rear of the building there are some empty trunks, a mildewed safety net, a yellowed* Washington Daily News *dated 1933, a wrinkled, dirty but still spangled costume, or part of it anyway. That's the Ward barn today.*[177]

A ray of hope for the barn came from Baraboo, Wisconsin, and its Circus World Museum, which had hopes of either dismantling it and reconstituting on its own grounds or reproducing a facsimile. Thankfully, for the sake of the historical record, workers from Circus World Museum took all the necessary measurements of the barn,[178] but the barn was eventually razed. No reproduction ever materialized in Baraboo.

The practice barn didn't survive, but the house at 1201 East Emerson, the former residence used by the Ward flyers, thrived for decades as a popular restaurant and tavern called the Grand Hotel. It was famous, at least in central Illinois, for its fried chicken, which was pan-fried and made to order. The décor of the restaurant was also well known; throughout it hung the memorabilia of Bloomington's circus past. It was originally operated as a bar by Frank De Valon, and husband-and-wife team Owen and Helen Benton began running the business as a restaurant in 1938.[179] The operation changed hands a number of times until it was finally demolished in 2002.[180]

There was always a good deal of speculation after the practice barn was destroyed that there must have been some unaccounted-for treasures of local circus memorabilia, either Ward or Concello in origin, that survived. For decades, this was at best only wishful thinking. But a fantastic revelation came to light in 2011 that changed all of that. Photographer and former Ringling Brothers and Barnum & Bailey clown Robert E. Handley, of Bloomington, had known in the 1960s that the barn's days were numbered and dutifully liberated a fantastic cache of Concello-era photographs, telegrams and wardrobe. This material had been the private collection of Art and Antoinette Concello, as evidenced by the numerous affectionately inscribed photographs from circus stars and friends, the likes of world-famous equestrian May Wirth and the unequalled master of trapeze Alfredo Codona, to name only two. Handley kept these historic items quietly tucked away in his possession for more than forty years until he felt that they should be included in the Circus and Allied Arts Collection at Illinois State University's Milner Library Special Collections. Shortly after Handley's visit to the barn, Circus World Museum personnel came to measure and photograph it. They also came away with a substantial number of historic items. Nine boxes of photographs, correspondence and other materials, again from the Concello era, reside in the museum's Robert L. Parkinson Library and Research Center.

THE LEGACY REMAINS

By the mid-1950s, Art Concello was entrenched in the management of circuses. He is credited with making the decision to centralize winter quarters in Sarasota. His doing so meant that the trapeze performers followed him there. As performers drifted away from central Illinois, a woman in the adjoining city of Normal strived to keep their legacy alive at the library of Illinois State Normal University.

Eleanor Weir Welch came to the university as its first professionally trained librarian and director in 1929. The daughter of a minister, she was used to traveling, but once she settled here, she never left. A spirited woman of character, Eleanor seemed to delight in providing the foundation for Special Collections, establishing three of them during her tenure: the Rare and Fine Book Collection, the Children's Literature Collection and the Circus and Allied Arts Collection.

The Circus and Allied Arts Collection started with the nucleus of donated scrapbooks and memorabilia from a number of Bloomington performers and other locals. Arnold Riegger, formerly of the Flying La Vans and longtime projectionist in the area's movie houses, donated a wealth of scrapbooks, photographs, letterheads and negatives detailing the Bloomington aerial scene in its glory days, when the vibrant Flying Wards were still captivating world audiences. Harold Ramage also donated several of his prized photo albums filled with autographed pictures affectionately inscribed to him by a host of circus royalty. Ramage was a great confidant and friend to Bloomington's circus folk and their trusted contact at millwright and welding outfit the Keiser-Van Leer Company. Keiser-Van Leer played an important role to aerialists by providing a wealth of specialty fittings and custom metalwork for their riggings. As the collection began to take shape and word started to spread, more materials began to be acquired that expanded its scope beyond Bloomington's circus heritage to universal coverage. Acquisition of both the Walter Scholl and Jo Van Doveren circus collections filled out an already rich resource even further.

The growth of the Circus and Allied Arts Collection caught the attention of noted circus fan, collector and historian Sverre O. Braathen in the mid-1960s. He and his wife, Faye, had amassed a magnificent collection of photographs, circus programs and route books. The Braathens had also corresponded with a wide variety of people associated with the circus, including legendary Ringling Brothers and Barnum & Bailey bandleader Merle Evans and Helen and Karl Wallenda of the Wallenda high-wire act.

Bloomington's the Flying Concellos on the Ringling Show in 1941, as seen through the prolifically snapping lens of Madison, Wisconsin attorney and well-known circus aficionado Sverre O. Braathen.

In many cases, this correspondence carried on for decades, giving incredible insight into the lives of circus folk. Throughout the 1930s, Braathen was also able to pull a phenomenal amount of material from the abandoned Ringling Circus winter quarters in Baraboo, Wisconsin, that had been slated for the fire pit. This archive paints a vivid picture of the circus from 1887 through 1921 with documentation such as financial ledgers, contracts correspondence, insurance forms, licenses, cancelled checks and invoices. Correspondence between the Ringling brothers themselves are a rich source of information about all facets of their operations. The Braathen Collection trickled into Milner Library during the last years of the couple's lives, but the largest portion of it was received after Faye passed away in 1976. Sverre had passed away in 1974.

Braathen, a Wisconsin attorney by trade but a circus enthusiast by blood, used photography as a way to gain friends in circus backyards throughout the American Midwest. He shot expensive Kodachrome images as early as 1941 at a number of circuses, eventually totaling roughly ten thousand images in rich, saturated color. Braathen's photographs made their international mass market debut in 2008, when they were featured in Taschen's 15.5-pound behemoth of a coffee table book titled *The Circus: 1870–1950* edited by Noel Daniel. The visual highpoints of the tome, Braathen's images have since been made available online via a permanent website called "A Passion for Circus" through Illinois State University's Milner Library. Since then, further exposure of Braathen's images and the Circus and Allied Arts Collection has come by way of the pages of the *New Yorker* and its online blog, ABC News online and the "Huffington Post," not to mention circus industry blogs like the very popular "Showbiz David" blog by noted author David Lewis Hammarstrom.

Further collections broadened the Circus and Allied Arts Collection over the years, such as the acquisition of the Al Dobritch Collection, which features correspondence, publicity materials and photographs. A bit like Art Concello, Dobritch had been a performer who transitioned into management, topping out as an agent for performers, a producer of Shrine circuses and a talent scout for MGM. His work ethic seemed to mirror that of Art Concello's. Asked if he ever took a vacation, Dobritch replied, "I planned to vacation on an island off the coast of Portugal, but after one

Equestrian extraordinaire Dorothy Herbert with the Cole Brothers Circus performing in Bloomington on July 23, 1941, as photographed by Sverre O. Braathen.

Iconic clowns Emmett Kelly (left) and Otto Griebling (center) with the Cole Brothers Circus playing Bloomington, Illinois, July 23, 1941, with journalist and author Earl Chapin May (right). Photographed by Sverre O. Braathen.

day, I was on the phone to New York. The circus," he continued, "is not a business; it's a disease."[181]

The efforts of the curator of the Circus and Allied Arts Collection, Steve Gossard, have, for a long period of heartbreaking community indifference, kept the circus story of the Twin Cities alive. Gossard's *A Reckless Era of Aerial Performance: The Evolution of Trapeze* is one of the few books written on the subject and is the only to cover its complex early years and evolution.

BLOOMINGTON, ILLINOIS...TRAPEZE CAPITAL AND MORE

Our initial hope in writing this book is to encourage the community of Bloomington-Normal to embrace its circus past and to continue to learn more about it. Though the scope of this book has been Bloomington-centric, the artists profiled helped influence and shape what the aerial arts are today. Their careers transcend mere local historical interest, and

"Pawnee Bill" Gordon Lillie may have been one of the last vestiges of the Old West, but he was also a native of the Twin Cities and a graduate of Bloomington High School (1879).

their accomplishments stand among the most astounding in the annals of circusdom. Bloomington-Normal has much to be proud of in this rich history of aerialists and impresarios. It impressed Pulitzer Prize–winning journalist and author Robert Lewis Taylor to write in his book *Center Ring*, "With the possible exception of Sarasota, Florida, Bloomington, Illinois contributed as much to the glamour of circuses as any other town in the world."[182]

While researching for this book, many more performers and characters came to light who fell outside our subject area. The Twin Cities were home to world-famous opera singers (Minnie Saltzman Stevens), staple of the sideshow World's Fattest Man (not really, but Baby Bliss was pretty big), scores of clowns, Old West icons (Bloomington High School graduate "Pawnee Bill," aka Gordon Lillie, partner of Buffalo Bill and showman in his own right), minstrel shows (Harry Robinson, "the man with the silver horn," of Harry Robinson's Minstrels, committed suicide in a Bloomington hotel room in 1889 once his life had crumbled),[183] winter quarters to shows (Kennedy Bros. Circus and Wild West Show), circus musicians (longtime circus cornetist Charles Browning), leading men of the New York stage (Elmer Buffam), writers (playwright Rachel Crothers and novelist Harold Sinclair) and even the gold standard of duck comedians (George Wills)![184] Each and every new name that surfaces calls out for further investigation, as they are pieces to the larger puzzle of "Why Bloomington?" Aerialists were simply the most prominent feature of what was a thriving and complicated community of performers and creative minds of all stripes. The Twin Cities continue to fascinate, and we assure you, their history is worth your time to delve into even further.

Notes

Chapter 1

1. L. Peter Molineux, correspondence to "Trapeze Flying School," dated June 21, 1957 (original document held in the Illinois State University, Special Collections, Milner Library, Circus and Allied Arts Collection).

Chapter 2

2. *Daily Pantagraph*, "Items," September 22, 1877, 4.
3. *New York Clipper*, "Master Howard LaVan," February 16, 1878, 375.
4. *New York Clipper*, "Pullman and Hamilton's Show," July 6, 1878, 119.
5. *Chicago Daily Tribune*, "The Olympic," April 2, 1880, 12.
6. *Indiana Weekly Messenger* [Indiana, PA], "The Big Show Coming," May 19, 1880, 3.
7. *New York Clipper*, "Fredericks and Gloss Brothers," January 11, 1879, 331.
8. *New York Clipper*, "Dr. Thayer's Great Show and United Aggregation," August 21, 1880, 171.
9. *Boston Daily Globe*, "For a Life and Other Howard Attractions," December 11, 1881, 9; *Evening Courier and Republic* [Buffalo, NY], "Lang's Adelphi," April 1, 1884.
10. *Daily Inter Ocean*, "Bloomington," September 2, 1888.
11. *Anaconda Standard* [Anaconda, MT], "Society," July 10, 1904, 6.

12. *Daily Pantagraph* [Bloomington, IL], "Bloomington 'Flyers'...," July 22, 1928, 1.

13. *Boston Herald*, "Stage Matters, Notes," February 22, 1894, 8.

14. *Centralia Enterprise and Tribune* [Centralia, WI], "News Paragraphs," August 25, 1894, 11.

15. *Logansport Pharos* [Logansport, IN], "City News," August 17, 1894, 3.

16. *The Sun* [New York, NY], "The Circus Has Come to Town," July 17, 1895, 7.

17. *New Orleans Times Picayune*, "LaVans of Flying Trapeze Celebrate Golden Wedding," December 21, 1945, 29.

18. Ibid.

19. *Daily Pantagraph*, "Fred Green Is Dead," June 15, 1897, 7.

20. *New York Clipper*, "Under the Tents," April 30, 1898, 145.

21. Kenneth Silverman, *Houdini!: The Career of Erich Weiss: American Self-Liberator, Europe's Eclipsing Sensation, World's Handcuff King & Prison Breaker* (New York: HarperCollins, 1996), 34–35.

22. *New York Dramatic Mirror*, "Vaudeville Correspondence, Kansas City," May 6, 1899, 22.

23. *The Freeman* [Indianapolis, IN], "Notes from the Campbell Bros.' Consolidated Shows," October 3, 1903, 6.

24. *Daily Pantagraph*, "Bloomington 'Flyers'...," July 22, 1928, 1.

Chapter 3

25. *Daily Pantagraph*, "Fred Multimore [*sic*] Acrobat, Visits Old Home," June 30, 1910, 7.

26. *New York Clipper*, "Maxwell & Smith's Great Western Sensation," April 17 (Supplement), 1875; *Daviess County Democrat* [Washington, IN], Advertisement, September 25, 1875, 1. This circus can be found alternatively advertised under the name of Maxwell and Smith's Great Western Sensation Shows.

27. *Quincy Daily Whig*, "Local Miscellany," April 29, 1884, 8.

28. *Quincy Daily Journal*, "Forepaugh Coming," June 25, 1887, 4.

29. *Billboard*, "Under the Marquee," November 21, 1914, 23.

30. *Daily Bulletin* [Bloomington, IL], "In Memory of a Loved Friend," September 11, 1910, 2.

31. Clyde V. Noble, "Bloomington, Illinois the Home of 'The Man on the Flying Trapeze'" (unpublished manuscript, later published with few changes in *White Tops* 23, no. 9–10 [1950]).

32. *Daily Pantograph*, "Local Couple's Experience Reads Like a Story Book," November 14, 1937, 14.

33. Ibid.

34. *Billboard*, "The Final Curtain," December 28, 1940, 128.

Chapter 4

35. *Atlanta Argus* [Atlanta, IL], "Atlanta Fair," September 3, 1903.

36. Earl C. May, "A Single Slip Means Death to Eddie Ward's Pupils," *Popular Science*, May 1926, 31–32, 133.

37. *Lawrence* [KS] *Daily World*, "Girl from Abilene," October 3, 1904, 4.

38. *San Antonio Daily Light*, "The Parker Pike," March 26, 1905, 9

39. *Daily Republican* [Fort Scott, KS], "Tiny Girl with Nerve, Miss Jennie Ward Does Many Daring Stunts," July 14, 1905, 1.

40. *Waterloo Evening Courier*, "'Flying Wards' in Circus Train Wreck from Troy Mills," June 26, 1918, 2.

41. *Cedar Rapids Gazette*, "World-Famous Trapeze Actors Give Show for the Home Folk," December 4, 1914, 25.

42. *Waterloo Times Tribune*, "At the Majestic," February 7, 1913, 7.

43. *Cedar Rapids Evening Gazette*, "Star Aerial Performers Are Linn County Residents," March 19, 1913, 3.

44. *Daily Pantagraph*, "Famous 'Flying Wards' Are Training Hard for Opening of Show Season," March 6, 1925, 14.

45. Hugh C. Weir, "Women of the Circus," *Hampton's Magazine*, 1909, 797–805.

46. *Billboard*, "Sawdust and Tinsel," August 19, 1911, 26

47. *Grand Island Independent*, "Actress Falls Long Distance; Thrilling Incident Stirred Spectators at Circus Yesterday," August 4, 1911, 1.

48. *Daily Bulletin*, "Says Engineer Was Not in Cab—Flagman of Circus Train—Declares Nobody Was Visible When He Threw Fuse Through Cab," June 24, 1918, 1.

49. *Daily Pantagraph*, "Bloomington's Famous Acrobatic Troupe Is Invaded by Death," June 24, 1918, 3.

50. *Daily Bulletin*, "Eddie Ward, Supreme Aerialist, Braves Dangers of Trade for Fun There's in It," December 4, 1927, 1B.

Chapter 5

51. *Daily Pantagraph*, "Coliseum—Third Annual Traveling Men's Minstrels," February 7, 1902, 7.

52. *Daily Pantagraph*, "Indoor Circus a Big Success," January 3, 1910, 9.

53. *Daily Pantagraph*, "All Ready for Circus," March 25, 1915, 5.

54. *Daily Pantagraph*, "The Indoor Circus," January 22, 1901, 7.

55. Ibid.

56. *Daily Pantagraph*, "Carnival of Athletics," January 1, 1904, 5.

57. *Daily Bulletin*, "New Year Crowds Attend Circus," January 3, 1910, 13.

58. *Daily Pantagraph*, "Indoor Circus Again Pleases Spectators," January 2, 1910, 9.

59. *Daily Pantagraph*, "Indoor Circus a Big Success."

60. *Daily Pantagraph*, "'Y' Circus" Advertisement, March 21, 1925, 6; *Daily Pantagraph*, "YMCA Circus a Decided Success," March 25, 1926, 7.

61. *Daily Pantagraph*, "Annual YM Circus Opens Today," March 23, 1931, 3.

62. *Daily Pantagraph*, "First Productions of 'Y' Annual Circus Given Yesterday," March 25, 1926, 7.

63. *Daily Pantagraph*, "YMCA Annual Circus Opens with True 'Big Top' Atmosphere," March 24, 1931, 3.

64. *Daily Pantagraph*, "Circus Signs Notable Act," March 17, 1934, 3.

65. *Daily Pantagraph*, "Circus Opens Stand Tonight," March 26, 1935, 14.

66. *Daily Pantagraph*, "Bilettis Sign for 'Y' Circus," March 23, 1937, 10.

67. Milton Bleumke, "Circus Makes History at 'Y,'" *Daily Pantagraph*, March 24, 1936, 3.

68. *Daily Pantagraph*, "Blonde Ulaine to Perform in Circus, Aerial Artist Likes Annual Show Here," March 15, 1936, 3.

69. *Daily Pantagraph*, "YMCA Annual Circus Opens with True…," n.d., 3.

70. *Daily Pantagraph*, "Puts Lions through Paces Here—Soft Words Coax Restless Lions as They Eye New Surroundings," March 20, 1940, 3.

71. *Daily Pantagraph*, "Amateurs, Professionals to Join Tonight for Annual 'Y' Circus," March 12, 1932, 3.

72. *Daily Pantagraph*, "Boys' Troupe on Program—YMCA Youths to Present Pyramid Act at Circus Next Week," March 25, 1937, 13.

73. *Daily Pantagraph*, "Thrill Packed Show Planned by YMCA—Annual Show Opens Monday for a Week," March 23, 1940, 3.

74. James Monahan, "Interview with Harold Ramage" (unpublished manuscript dated March 29, 1957, held at Illinois State University, Special Collections, Milner Library, Circus and Allied Arts Collection).

75. *Daily Pantagraph*, "Great Array of Talent to Give Circus Thrills," March 23, 1941, 3.

76. James Monahan, "Interview with Harry Melby" (unpublished manuscript dated April 18, 1957, held at Illinois State University, Special Collections, Milner Library, Circus and Allied Arts Collection).

77. A.M. Jackson to Art Concello, letter printed on State Farm letterhead dated February 24, 1944, and held in the Art Concello Papers, Robert L. Parkinson Library, Circus World Museum, Baraboo, Wisconsin.

78. *Daily Pantagraph*, "Aerialist's Lament—Mickey King Finds Old Stand Changed," March 22, 1957, 3.

79. Fred A. Hacker and P.W. Eames, *How to Put on an Amateur Circus* (Chicago: T.S. Denison & Company, 1923), 5.

80. *Spokane Press*, "Y.M.C.A. Circus Is the Most Magnificent of Modern Times," March 20, 1910, 24.

81. Charles W. Fairbanks, "Address of Vice President Fairbanks. Laying of the Corner Stone of the Y.M.C.A., Bloomington, September 22, 1907" (unpublished document held in the archives at the Bloomington YMCA), 2.

Chapter 6

82. John B. Freed, *Educating Illinois: Illinois State University, 1857–2007* (Virginia Beach, VA: Donning Co. Publishers, 2009), 179.

83. Ibid., 160.

84. Clifford Horton to his son, December 4, 1943 (held at Illinois State University, Special Collections, Milner Library, Circus and Allied Arts Collection, Gamma Phi Circus Archive).

85. Pricilla L. Gilroy, "The Development of Gamma Phi Honorary Gymnastic Fraternity from 1929 to 1975," 8, written as a course requirement for HPER 475 at Illinois State University (held at Illinois State University, Special Collections, Milner Library, Circus and Allied Arts Collection, Gamma Phi Circus Archive).

86. Ibid., 10.

87. Tom De Carlo, *Handbook of Progressive Gymnastics* (Englewood Cliffs, NJ: Prentice Hall, 1963), 228.

88. *Ohio Wesleyan Transcript*, "Gamma Phi," December 12, 1917, 2.

89. Gilroy, "Development of Gamma Phi," 9.

90. *Ohio Wesleyan Transcript*, "Athletic Carnival of February 22 Measures Up to Former Standard," February 27, 1918, 3.

91. *Vidette*, "Gamma Phi, New Fraternity Meets," November 11, 1929, 3.

92. Gilroy, "Development of Gamma Phi," 11.

93. Telephone interview with Cliff E. Horton, March 5, 2013.

94. Gilroy, "Development of Gamma Phi," 29.

95. Ibid., 17.

96. *Spectacle*, "A Small Town in Illinois Has Turned Out to Be Anything but Normal" (Fall 1999): 28.

97. "Gamma Phi Circus Program," 1956, 2.

98. Letter from Roy Moore, charter member, to Bill Jaeger, December 4, 1982 reproduced in unpublished manuscript by William Jaeger, Gamma Phi historian (held at Illinois State University, Special Collections, Milner Library, Circus and Allied Arts Collection, Gamma Phi Circus Archive).

99. Clifford Horton, phone interview by Maureen Brunsdale, Colorado Springs, CO, March 21, 2013.

Chapter 7

100. Robert L. Taylor, *Center Ring: The People of the Circus* (New York: Doubleday, 1956), 167.

101. Ibid., 168.

102. Tom Parkinson, "A 1973 Interview with Art Concello," *Bandwagon*, September–October 2001, 7.

103. Taylor, *Center Ring*, 169–70.

104. Ibid., 170.

105. *Times Picayune*, "Pretty Trapeze Artist Showing Girls the Ropes," July 23, 1972, sec. 4, 11.

106. Transcript of Art Concello interview by George Brinton Beal for Radio Station WORL, Wednesday, May 4 [no year stated], 2 (MS Thr 675 (11), held at Harvard Theatre Collection, Houghton Library, Harvard University).

107. Parkinson, "1973 Interview," 7.

108. *Daily Pantagraph*, "Vasconcellos, Local Aerialist, Marries," June 9, 1929, 3A.

109. Transcript, Concello/Beal, 4.

110. *Daily Pantagraph*, "Concellos Buys Famous Ward Estate for Training Aerialists," August 4, 1935, 9.

111. Transcript, Concello/Beal, 4.

112. Bill Ballantine, "Damnedest Showman Since Barnum," *Cavalier*, October 1957, 34.

113. Raymond Toole Stott, "That Daring Young Woman on the Flying Trapeze," *Sawdust Ring*, January–March 1935, 9.

114. Thomas Allen, "Girl on the Flying Trapeze," *Maclean's Magazine*, May 1, 1953, 68.

115. Emma Jane Riley, "Trapeze Capital," *Illinois Quest* 2, no. 1 (1940): 20.

116. *Sheboygan Press*, "'Greatest Show on Earth' Proves Right to Its Title at Two Performances Here," August 14, 1937, 2.

117. Transcript, Concello/Beal, 11.

118. *Milwaukee Journal Green Sheet*, "Big Boss of Big One Started Career on the Flying Trapeze," September 27, 1949, 1.

119. Transcript, Concello/Beal, 9.

120. 1931 Diary, Art Concello Papers, Robert L. Parkinson Library, Circus World Museum.

121. Ballantine, "Damnedest Showman," 34.

122. Ted Landale, "D---dest Showman Since P.T. Barnum," *Sunday World-Herald* [Omaha, NE], August 10, 1958, 8F.

123. 1934–35 Diary, Art Concello Papers, Robert L. Parkinson Library, Circus World Museum.

124. *Billboard*, "R-B Circus Goes Back to Barn When Majority Refuses 25% Cut," July 2, 1938, 65.

125. Henry Ringling North and Arlen Hatch, *The Circus Kings: Our Ringling Family Story* (Gainesville: University Press of Florida, 2008), 285.

126. Parkinson, "1973 Interview," 11.

127. Ibid.

128. Joseph L. Myler, "World's Greatest Trainer of Circus Aerialists but 29," *Oshkosh Northwestern*, April 16, 1940, 5.

129. *The Aegis*, Bloomington High School yearbook, 1926, 87.

Chapter 8

130. *Billboard*, "RB Given 'Theater' Tinge," April 18, 1942, 3.

131. *Billboard*, "Over 40 RB Animals Burn," August 15, 1942, 38, 46.

132. *Billboard*, "Robert Ringling Heads RB; John R. North Is Out as Prexy; Smith Replaces Concello as Mgr; 1943 Tour Certain Says Butler," January 23, 1943, 36.

133. *Billboard*, "Dressing Room Gossip," August 21, 1943, 39.

134. *Evening World Herald* [Omaha, NE], "Booking Agent Buys Russell Bros. Circus," July 1, 1943, 16; *San Diego Union*, "Suit Reveals Breakup of Circus Partnership," December 8, 1943, 8B.

135. *San Diego Union*, "Suit Reveals Breakup."

136. Chang Reynolds, "Clyde Beatty and Russell Bros. Combined Circus, Season of 1944," *Bandwagon*, May–June 1969, 10–19.

137. *Billboard*, "What Will Artie Do? Speculation Mounts on Concello's Future," December 19, 1953, 62.

138. *Russell Bros. Pan-Pacific Circus—Circus Magazine and Digest*, 1945.

139. *Billboard*, "What Will Artie Do?"

140. *Billboard*, "North Launches R-B Revamp; Concello Now General Mgr.," November 29, 1947, 69, 139.

141. *Billboard*, "R-B Seattle Biz Socko," September 4, 1948, 60.

142. *Billboard*, "What Will Artie Do?"

143. *Daily Pantagraph*, "Circus Museum Gets Model of Twin Citian's Invention," May 22, 1960, 8.

144. *Dallas Morning News*, "Streamlining Show Is Job of Concello," September 22, 1948, sec. II, 5; *Billboard*, "North Revamp."

145. *Billboard*, "What Will Artie Do?"

146. Ibid.

147. *Newport Daily News*, "Controlling Circus Interest Sold by Clyde Beatty," January 6, 1955, 9.

148. *Odessa American*, "Artists' Strike Closes Circus," May 11, 1956, 32.

149. *Deming* [NM] *Headlight*, "Beatty Circus Property Will Be Sold Under Foreclosure," June 29, 1956, 1.

150. *Dallas Morning News*, "Ringling Bros. Circus Restores Train for Annual Show," September 18, 1960, sec. 5, 1.

151. *Billboard*, "Ringling Minority Appears United, Ready for Action," July 8, 1957, 58.

152. *Billboard*, "Ringling Selling Equipment; Writs Denied; Home Sold," March 3, 1958, 62.

153. *Billboard*, "49ers Withdraw Last Lawsuit Against North," June 13, 1960, 51.

154. David L. Hammarstrom, *Big Top Boss: John Ringling North and the Circus* (Urbana: University of Illinois Press, 1992), 209–11.

Chapter 9

155. *Evening Independent* [Massillon, OH], "Noted Denver Aerialist Coming Here with Sells-Floto Circus," undated clipping in the Doss Family Scrapbook, Illinois State University, Special Collections, Milner Library, Circus and Allied Arts Collection.

156. *Glimmerglass* [Cooperstown, NY], "Downie Bros. Big Circus Here Today," August 1928.

157. *Goshen* [IN] *Weekly News Times*, "Elkhart Relative Gets Word from Performers," June 28, 1918, 5.

158. *Daily Twin Falls* [ID] *Times*, "Sixty Circus People Killed in Collision," June 22, 1918, 1.

159. *Spartanburg* [SC] *Herald Journal*, "Shows, Acts Are Booked for Fair," October 2, 1935, 6.

160. Evelyn Simpson, correspondence with Steve Gossard, dated June 14, 1986; original document held in Gossard's collected research materials, Illinois State University, Special Collections, Milner Library, Circus and Allied Arts Collection.

161. *Billboard*, "Brush Fire Fatal to Rose Woeckener," April 6, 1946, 72.

162. *Billboard*, "Talent Topics," November 10, 1951, 61.

163. *Daily Pantagraph*, "Hendryx Funeral to Be Held Sunday," March 8, 1939, 3.

164. *Daily Pantagraph*, "W.F. 'Happy' Hunt, Hotel Man, Dies at 80," May 20, 1964, 3.

165. *Billboard*, "Shavings from the Sherman," December 14, 1946, 69.

166. *Billboard*, "Polack Eastern Unit," February 3, 1951, 51.

167. *Billboard*, "Mickey King Internationally Renowned Aerialist," November 2, 1935, cover.

168. *Fowler Benton Review*, "Big Free Circus at Kankakee Fair," August 27, 1914, 5.

169. Charles Ringling correspondence to Bert Lafayette, October 17, 1916, original document held in the Pfening Archives.

170. *Billboard*, "Marriages—Thornton-Lafayette," October 28, 1916, 51.

171. *Manitoba Free Press*, "Music and Drama," March 12, 1915, 10.

172. Art Monette's Scrapbook, original document held in Illinois State University, Special Collections, Milner Library, Circus and Allied Arts Collection.

173. *Delmarva Star* [Wilmington, DE], "Battle of Blond Charmers Menaces Max Baer's Hard-Fought-for Bankroll," March 11, 1934, 23.

174. *Huntingdon Daily News* [Huntingdon County, PA], advertisement, August 5, 1927, 8.

175. *Billboard*, "George Valentine Establishes Circus Haven at Normal, Ill.," January 10, 1948, 45.

Chapter 10

176. *Daily Pantagraph*, "Bloomington Seeks to Attract Circus Acts," December 31, 1939, 3.

177. *Daily Pantagraph*, "Famed Circus Barn Nearing End," November 14, 1965, 44.

178. Ibid.

179. *Daily Pantagraph*, "Grand Hotel Famous for Flyers, Chicken," April 28, 1976, 28.

180. *Daily Pantagraph*, "Grand Hotel Razed," June 27, 2002, 1.

181. *Milwaukee Journal Green Sheet*, "Circus Boss Tailors the Acts to Fit the Tastes of the Towns," February 17, 1965, 1.

182. Taylor, *Center Ring*, 67.

183. *New York Times*, "Suicide of a Former Minstrel," May 6, 1889, 1.

184. *Rockford Daily Register*, "Acrobats in Bloomington for Winter," December 18, 1923, 9.

INDEX

About the Authors

Maureen Brunsdale became the Special Collections and Rare Books librarian at Illinois State University in the summer of 2008. There, she oversees four magnificent collections—none more intriguing and enchanting than the Circus & Allied Arts Collection. She is a member of both the Circus Fans Association and the Circus Historical Society, serving as a board member for the latter. She has an undergraduate degree from St. Olaf College and master degrees from the University of Iowa and the University of South Dakota.

Mark Schmitt is a lifelong native of Bloomington, Illinois, and a graduate of Illinois State University with a bachelor's degree in English. Having trod the very same high school hallways as Art Concello and "Tuffy" Genders, it is fitting that Milner Library's Circus and Allied Arts Collection called out to him, where he is a senior specialist in Special Collections and Rare Books.